E- English Grammar

E- English Grammar

Grammar

Vol. - I

Durga Prasad

PARTRIDGE

ISBN:	Hardcover	978-1-4828-8394-7
	Softcover	978-1-4828-8393-0
	eBook	978-1-4828-8392-3

Print information available on the last page.

To order additional copies of this book, contact
Partridge India
000 800 10062 62
orders.india@partridgepublishing.com

www.partridgepublishing.com/india

Contents

Dedication

In Memory of My Mother

Late Ram Dulari Devi
(Expired on 5th Jan. 1988)

Preface

English is an international language. People all over the world are desirous of learning this language. Language is learnt either at home or in school. The language which is learnt at home is termed as "Mother Language." It is the mother that teaches her child for the first time. It is the mother that gives birth to a baby - male or female, nourishes him/her and teaches him or her how to recognise the person, place or thing in and around him or her. The medium through which mother explains in her tiny broken word/words so that the child can grasp (pick up) at ease and understand it thoroughly is said to be the language in real sense of the term. English is the mother language or tongue of the English who originally hail from any part of the country and territories under the jurisdiction and rule of the Great Britain. Slowly and slowly the British under its ruler so called king or queen started evading the nearby countries and began to rule over them for a pretty long time. Likewise the number of such small territory went on increasing and within a few decades the British ruled almost all over the world. As the earth is round the Sun rises in one part of it - it is known as day while sets in another part of it - it is known as night. We normally know where the Sunlight prevails, it is called day and where darkness prevails, it is called night. A time came in the history of British regime that almost all countries said to be the territories around the world were under their rule and administration. People used to say that the Sun never set during the period of the British Regime.

Obviously, where the British ruled over, English became the official language and consequently the people under their control had to learn English language and literature in order to get a better job. Moreover English was made compulsory subjects in schools, colleges, institutions and universities.

As such a large number of missionaries were opened in main cities and towns of so called territories where the weaker class of society was admitted, fed and brought up free of cost. They were taught by the nun primarily English language to read, write and speak. The very purpose of such missionaries was to help the unprivileged and downtrodden people. With the pace of time from the grass root levels of primary, middle and high schools English was taught to the students from the very beginning. At matriculation and entrance levels all the subjects of the syllabus or curriculum were in English and to get through all these two examinations viz. matriculation and entrance one had to be strong, if not versed in or mastery over English language and literature. There are two more important reasons for learning English - the first almost all the books of the prescribed syllabus were available in English only and the secondly those who were at par or superior to the British in qualification were getting opportunity of better services or jobs also in Government company or in their offices.

After so many centuries the people of the territories so ruled by the British raised their voice for freedom, fought and became independent, these territories became democratic countries like our country - India (Bharat) but the craze of English language and literature has not decreased rather has increased tremendously in most of such countries other things being equal.

The reasons are quite obvious. In higher education like science and technology, medical and engineering, commerce and trade, business management and administration the syllabi are taught in English only. The books also are available in English only.

Now the countries whose mother tongue is not English, English is used as second language or so of the state. All prestigious examinations are conducted in English only. That is why English is a must, if anyone wants to go up in career so to say in life.

We got freedom on 15th. August 1947 and started ruling the country democratically on and from 26th. January 1950 when our constitution was promulgated and became effective all over the country. In order to commemorate these two auspicious days, we Indians celebrate them as Independence Day on 15th. August and 26th. January as Republic Day every year. These two days are the national holidays all over the country and we celebrate them as our national festivals. Our national flags are hoisted in all Govt. and Non- Govt. offices, schools, colleges, universities, organisations and so on by the dignitaries.

Whatever has been said above is only the history about how English language became so important as well as prominent in all over the countries or territories of the globe wherein the British rules were prevalent and the people had to obey the law of the land in the right spirit and letters.

Now I do come to the point. The book in your hand is an English grammar written by me in a very simple language with suitable examples explaining appropriately pros and crones of the subject in question so that the readers of grass root level, middle level as well as of higher level can grasp (pick up), can understand and can learn English particularly how to read, write and speak English correctly with ease.

Only the important chapters of English grammar have been explained with suitable examples. The main chapters are as follows:

1. Orthography
2. Etymology
3. Sentence
4. Kinds of Sentence
5. Parts of Speech
6. Analysis of Sentence
7. Analysis (Principal Clause and Subordinate Clause)
8. Synthesis
9. Transformation of Sentence
10. Voice Change
11. Degree Change
12. Narration
13. Verb
14. Adverb
15. Preposition
16. Conjunction
17. Interjection
18. Punctuation

Do hope this book will prove to be an asset, moreover a guide, not only to the students but their parents and teachers also.

Its second volume or part will be available within a very short period of time from the date of publication of this book which will cover the rest chapters of Grammar. English Grammar is a tough subject and to write it suitably is tougher than anything else.

The book in question is the outcome of my effort sincerely made during the period of the last five decades in teaching English language and literature to the pupils of different levels of schools and colleges particularly when I had been an Assistant Teacher of English and later on generally when I was employed with different firms & companies in different posts & positions. Since it was my hobby to teach English language & literature, I used to teach my wards & the wards of my colleagues as and when I got time. After superannuation I thought of writing books on English language & literature so that the people residing in different corners of the world can be in a position to learn it with ease.

Since the e-classes were taken exclusively through computers, all the chapters were saved as treasure and preserved in the Hard Disk. Now after a pretty long time my daughter Mrs. Susmita Bharti M.Sc. (Zoology), B.Ed., B.T.C., Assistant Teacher, Varanasi requested me to make the whole chapters, which were taught to my grandsons and granddaughters, make available in a book form inasmuch as she needs the book urgently to learn herself and also to teach her students.

I assessed, planned properly and lastly succeeded in making it in a book form to her entire satisfaction. My grandson - Mr. Shubham Kumar who is now a student of Asansol Engineering College, West Bengal and my granddaughter - Miss Monika Kumari who is now a student of B.P. Poddar Institute of Management and Technology, West Bengal helped me a lot in searching, setting and consolidating the whole matters of what I had taught them nearly a few years back. I am thankful to them in assisting in my work.

I am also thankful to Mr. Jairam Rajwar - a senior teacher of English for his valuable guidance and assistance extended to me in completing the book.

I am grateful to Late Santosh Kumar Banerji and Late Ramakant Jha - formerly Headmaster and Assistant Headmaster respectively for teaching me English in my school days.

Durga Prasad.
Govindpur, Dhanbad, Jharkhand - 828109.
Mahashivaratri,
7th. March 2016 (Monday)
Mob.Nos: 9304885187/9430730717
E-Mail: durga.prasad.1946@gmail.com
Website - www.e-bluebooks.com

E – ENGLISH GRAMMAR (ORTHOGRAPHY ONLY)

Description (Orthography)

"HOW TO TEACH AND LEARN ENGLISH" is a major subject in which the author has made an attempt to explain as to how effectively and efficiently the students of nursery classes at the primary level of education the first chapter of English Grammar termed as **"ORTHOGRAPHY"** can be taught step by step.

In this chapter students are taught alphabet – a group of 26 letters of English language – Capital and Small letters both separately step by step.

The author has suggested the important method and procedure how nicely with ease the children in between the age groups of 3 to 5 years can be taught in their classes by their class teachers and at home by their parents as well.

Children at this age are very sensitive to grasp (pick up) the subject concerned and as such they should be taught with sheer love and affection so that fear or hesitation does not enter their heart or mind about the teachers or parents in any way, in any shape or form.

Regular practice of reading and writing can strengthen their aptitude or attitude of learning their lessons quickly and improving their performance to a higher quality/standard. It is to be taken care of.

The author has suggested for holding the regular tests/examinations based on the lesson taught to them so that the result of individual performance can be known and corrective measures can be taken to improve the shortcomings, if any, found in any of the students. Teacher and parents meet should be arranged by the school authority to interact on the periodical progress of their wards.

The parents must take care of their children. They should spare some time regularly in teaching their lessons, they should not depend totally upon their class teachers/schools. The role of parents in building the career of their wards at the very initial stage of education, in any way, is of no less important than that of the class teachers.

Durga Prasad.
Author

*   *   *

ORTHOGRAPHY

English grammar is divided into five parts:

1. Orthography
2. Etymology
3. Syntax
4. Punctuation and
5. Prosody

ORTHOGRAPHY: Orthography can be defined as a method or system of how rightly one can learn to write, read and speak out (pronounce) the letters of the language concerned (here English Language as referred above). From the true sense of the term it is an art as well as a science. It is a technique how nicely it can be written with ease and how correctly can be read out.

In fact it is the initial chapter which teaches us about 26 letters of English language – the group of which is known as alphabet. Alphabet is reckoned as the cluster of these 26 letters and again all these 26 letters are either vowels or consonant.

Vowels are of five kinds whereas the rest of the 21 letters are called consonant

A, E, I, O, and U are 5 vowels whereas the rest of 21 letters B, C, D, F, G, H, J, K, L, M, N, P, Q, R, S, T, V, W, X, Y, and Z are 21 consonants.

5 vowels and 21 consonants – altogether 26 letters are jointly termed as Alphabet. Alphabet is nothing but a group of 26 letters beginning with A and ending in Z.

Thus Orthography is the most important chapter in which children of nursery classes or any learners of any other language can get acquainted with all these 26 letters. It is the base ladder that leads one in learning up to the top level, here that anyone succeeds means succeeds like success in learning it for his/her better prospect.

Once again these 26 letters are written in two ways - one is known as CAPITAL LETTERS and another as SMALL LETTERS.

At the very initial or at the beginning of education so to say at primary level of education the students are taught to recognize each and every letter in CAPITAL LETTERS from A to Z and secondly how to

write them in their slates or copies with pencils or pens (preferably ball pens) only.

The next stage of teaching to teach them to pronounce all these letters correctly, and after that the question of teaching them small letters arises. Similarly the students are asked to recognize each letter one by one and also taught how nicely and conveniently these letters can be written on their slates or copies – the methods and procedures of writing the letters in a right direction using the straight and curved lines is taught to the students step by step.

The teacher himself or herself must know the art of writing these letters and also must know the technique as to how easily and nicely with sheer patience can be taught to his or her students within the prescribed period of time – in between 3 to six months. Here the teachers have to be cool and quit to teach their students who have tiny hands with tender fingers. The aptitude and attitude of the students at the learning stage differ from one to another, inasmuch as the art of writing is considered as an inborn quality of the students – some students grasp quickly and learn within a very short period of time whereas some take much more period of time in learning. The second most important aspect or part that a few students write the letters very beautifully that attract the attention of the teachers or anybody who happens to see their writing – so good handwriting – good handwriting whereas in some students this quality is lacking and they write the letters absurdly and then we say their handwriting is not up to the desired level or up to the mark or up to the desired standard, instead we use to remark it as not good hand - writing or as bad hand - writing. Here the teachers have to pay more attention to such children and teach them with sheer patience with immense love and affection the art or technique to improve their hand writing – the students of such category are to be practised again and again and instead of scolding them should be encouraged or motivated in the ways they need or require. I think their parents particularly the mothers are to be contacted and are to be informed about the performance of their wards in class and also requested to take care of the weaknesses of their wards.

As the mother is the first teacher of her babies, she can be better utilised to improve the shortfalls of their wards. The mothers should co - operate the teachers in strengthening the foundation of their wards. It is such a period – let it be a critical one, when much more care is to be taken by school teachers as well as the parents to improve the students lacking in and naturally lagging behind in their classes, the unforeseen part attributable to spoil the students is their shyness in the company of their good colleagues and performing better than them. **Such shyness in the long run deviates the students in question from the study and gradually day by day they lose interest in learning their lessons.**

What I have seen and marked in most of the schools in primary classes like nursery, KG- I and KG- II students are provided 4 lines ruled copies to write capital and small letters in order. **The method or procedure to write these capital and small letters are to be taught to the students as to which lines are to be better used for which letters or alphabets.**

For instance all upper three lines are to be used in writing the capital letters from A to Z.

But in case of small letters or alphabets there are four important methods to write all the small letters but quite differently:

Category **A: a, c, e, i, m, n, o, r, s, u, v, w, x, and z – total = 14 letters.**

These 15 small letters are to be written in between the two middle lines.

Category B: b,d, h, k, l and t = total 6 small letters are to be written in between the first three lines leaving the last below line untouched or unused.

Category C: g, j, q, and y = 4 small letters are to be written in between the last three lines leaving the first line untouched or unused.

Category D: f and p = total 2 small letters are to be written in between all the four lines from top to bottom.

If we add all the total small letters of all four categories from A to D, we find 26 letters in totality. Now the class teacher can understand as to how better these four lines can be utilized for a better result. **Once the students learn to write in accordance with the methods as explained above, it will be easier for them to grasp the technique which small letters are to be written better and how. Regular practice of writing will automatically change into their habit or nature of writing suitably as well as correctly.**

Proper care should be taken in selecting the teachers to teach the children in primary classes like nursery, KG- I and KG – II and so on ...

They should be preferably convent educated – their basic education should be from English medium school only. They should be at least matriculate – 10th passed with very good result. They should be of sober nature and of well behaviour. They must be calm and quit. They must have the patience to listen, patience to understand actually what her students expect from her to learn their lessons. They should teach them with ease and comfort.

At these levels of education the task of teachers coupled with the duty and responsibility is very important one inasmuch **as the career building of the students starts from here itself.**

It is no exaggeration to say that students' handwriting plays a very vital role as almost all the tests and examinations are conducted in black and white. The students are to answer the questions in answer books in writing. Hand writing must be fair, clear and eligible that can satisfy the examiners – to their eyes as well to their head and heart.

Guidelines to the parents of the kids/children/wards:

It is said and also true in the right sense of the term that mother is the first teacher of her babies/children, and as such she should take care of them in all that they require for their physical and mental growth and for that they must know the liking and disliking of their children. The habit, nature, taste, behaviour of the child differs from one to another. Here the role of mother appears to be very important as well as vital. They should mark actually what their babies prefer to eat and drink, what their babies like to play and with whom, where they want to go with and with whom? and so on… It is seen that the babies/ children in between the age group of 3 to 5 years prefer playing (It includes walking, running, jumping, rocking, climbing, quarrelling with the mates etc.) indoor games and outdoor games alone or/and with his playmates to reading at homes or schools. In fact they don't take interest in study. **The first and foremost duty of the parents is to arouse interest in their children to sit for a few hours regularly and teach them the primary lessons – letters and figures – how to get them by heart, how to recognize them, how to write them nicely on slates and copies.** At this age children are much more interested in drawing something in the slates or copies. Taking into their sheer interest in drawing the parents should come forward and teach them how to draw common things, birds, animals and beasts which/whom they see in and around them every now and then like apple, bat, cat, dog, glass, jar, kite, ball, egg, rat, the Sun, the Moon, the stars, trees, hut, house, wall clock and so on… Gradually the children start taking interest in drawing and in course of drawing can learn a lot of things and can fair in their classes as soon as they are admitted to school in the nursery classes.

When it is confirmed that the children are taking interest in learning, the parents should be more attentive than it is proper to teach them how

to write letters and figures – 26 capital letters first then 26 small letters – figures from 1 to 100. Before starting to teach the lesson the parents should take the help from geometry. The children should be taught as to how draw lines differently – straight lines, horizontal, perpendicular, curved, zigzag, crossed, from down to up and up to down, to right from left and vice versa. Then to draw circle, square, angle, triangle, right-angle etc. All these drawing practice can help the children a lot in learning and knowing how letters can be written at ease with fairness too.

The parents should behave with their children with cordial love and affection, they must not misuse their tongs and hands in scolding or beating them, once the fear enters in their mind the very purpose of teaching will be lost. They should behave so politely as good friends, not as foes, so that the fear or hesitation does not get place in their head or heart. It is my bitter experience that once such things happen, it becomes too difficult to reform such children at initial stage or at later stage of learning so to say in education.

At this tender age mind is extremely sensitive to grasp quickly any good or bad things. The physical as well as mental growth is at the higher rate of levels.

The teachers of the nursery classes are also advised to go through the step by step teaching process to be adopted in the right spirit and letter in order to building their foundation stronger so that they can perform excellently in their higher classes.

There should be regular guidance and supervision by the teachers and parents in respect of their children's performance in the classes. The school should arrange regularly after test or examination whatsoever it may be "Teachers and Parents Meet" and shortfalls/weaknesses should be pointed out with the suitable advice or guidelines for better performance.

Parents are reckoned as an important chain in between their children and their teachers.

The duty and responsibility of the parents are not over the moment their wards are admitted to a good school, rather are multiplied inasmuch as they have to keep a watch what they read, how they do in the classes. They must see the remarks of the class teacher in their school diaries daily and assist them in doing their homework. They must know the portions of the syllabus for each and every test or examination and get them well prepared by way of teaching, revising their lessons at home in school days as well as on holidays.

Once Swami Vivekanand said, "Great things are achieved only with great sacrifices."

As such the parents have to sacrifice a lot in building the career of their children and in my opinion why not from the beginning stage to avoid repentance in later stages?

Now the most important chapter of English Grammar i.e. –

"Orthography" comes to an end. Now up to the parents and teachers how much more benefit they can derive from this mini book, so called booklet exclusively on the first chapter of English Grammar – "ORTHOGRAPHY".

* * *

E – ENGLISH GRAMMAR (ETYMOLOGY ONLY)

Description (Etymology)

This is another important chapter of English Grammar in which the method (methodology) of joining one letter of the alphabet to another letter of the alphabet is taught to the students. It is emphasized by the teachers as well as the parents as to how nicely and correctly they can form the word/words but with a meaningful sense.

It is a practical aspect of teaching the students – the art how they can write the letter one after another and join them to form a meaningful word.

The teachers should sit with the students and with their own hand show the students how nicely one letter can be joined to another letter or letters one by one to form a word. Here also four lining copies should be used by the students and preferably should be written with pencils only.

The manner, or the fashion, the method or the system, the technique or the art the students follow or adopt in joining one letter to another should be watched attentively and if they adopt the wrong ways or method it is to be rectified and the correct method is to be taught to practise again and again till he/she learns the art of writing the letters and joining them fairly and correctly. In the relevant chapter of Etymology the author has guided as to how properly teachers and parents can teach the wards (students) and as to how rightly the students can learn to write and join the letters to form meaningful word/words.

Do hope the guidelines as given in the chapter of Etymology will help the teachers and the parents to teach their students/wards properly with ease.

Durga Prasad
Author

*　　*　　*

ETYMOLOGY

In the first chapter of grammar the most important portion has already been explained as to how nicely the students of the nursery classes can be taught step by step all 26 letters – capital and small letters separately – the method or system as to how fairly these letters can be written with ease.

Till now with the regular practice of writing, recognizing, reading and pronouncing the letters correctly the students must have mastery over the technique or art of the subject in question.

The next chapter termed as ETYMOLOGY is dealt with the formation of words – words that are meaningful in sense by joining one letter to another or more than one.

The very purpose of this chapter is to teach the students the method or system or art or technique as to how correctly a word is formed and as to how beautifully it can be written with ease. Here again the role of teachers is as important as that of the parents.

Usually in all classes the common words beginning with each and every letter from A to Z are taught to the students to get by heart by repetition and regular practice and then they are taught to write these words one by one in the prescribed copies of four lines. The students are to be taught the correct pronunciation of these words, their meaning, their usage etc.

For instance A for Apple, B for Ball, C for Cat, D for Dog and so on...

Their interest can be aroused in case the students are taught to speak out the words starting from A to Z in a rhythmic manner joyfully.

It is advised that only the common words of common nouns should be preferably taught to the students as these can be seen, touched and felt in and around the areas wherein the students live and study. The power of memory is automatically enhanced as soon as the students see the things with their own eyes, touch them with their own hands or fingers. The moment they speak out the relevant word, their mind starts recollecting the shape and size of the thing which they have happened to see with their own eyes recently or in the past and/or have touched with their own hands or fingers.

Proper attention should be paid to increase the word power (Vocabulary) of students by apprising them of at least 5 words for each letter. For instance A for Apple, A for Ant, A for Aeroplane, A for Actor, A for Album. B for Ball, B for Bat, B for Bag, B for Baby, B for Balloon.

By teaching this way the word stock of the students will tend to increase day by day and moreover the students will get much more interest in learning the various types of words at a time. Their confidence level in learning process will also go up.

In and around the house where the children live in there are a large number of things in bed rooms, in drawing rooms, in bathrooms, in kitchens, in gardens, in playgrounds and so on. Outside the house also we find many things. In our body there are more than hundred limbs – some are outside of our body and some are inside of our body. The parents watch the TV along with their children. Many things appear before our eyes when we see any serials, sports, cartoons and so on.

If we take interest in all these things, we can show the children and apprise them of the important things one by one with their usage in our day to day life. Let us start to teach our wards using the technique as advised above. I am confident there will be very good result and after a few weeks or months you will find your wards speaking the words off and on even while walking or playing in house or outside the house. You will find that your wards are taking much more interest in learning their lessons joyfully. Such students with proper and regular guidance by the parents besides their class teacher will succeed like success in their classes. When our wards perform excellently in their classes, we not only become happy but be proud of them also.

Let us start from our body itself. Some limbs we see with our eyes, can touch them, can feel their shape and size too. Further we can know their function also. If we know all these things, there should not be any confusion to teach our wards about them one by one. When we sit closer to our wards and teach them practically what is what it is but natural their curiosity to see, touch and feel the things will tend to go up.

For instance: 1 Head: We can show our head and can say to the child, "It is my head, it is your head. Every child has a head like this. Head is big as a football. Touch my head. Touch with your right hand. It is round. It is hard. Your head is also round but it is not as hard as my head is. Your head is soft. Its skin is also soft. My head has hairs. These are hairs. These are black in colour. These are long. Your hair are not black. Your hairs are brown. Your hairs are short. We comb our hairs every day. We keep our head and hairs clean. Your mother's hairs are very long. They are very black. We use shop to wash our head and hairs. Your mother use shampoo.

2 Eyes: These are my eyes. You have your own eyes. We see with our eyes. We see many things. Here are a chair and a table. Touch each one after another. That is a fan. That is a bulb. That is a tube light. That is a door. That is a window. That is a television. It is a remote control. We can switch on or switch off our television with it. This is my pen. I write with it. You have a pencil. You write with it. And so on.....

All these things are useful. We see all these things with our eyes. I close my eyes like this. You can close your eyes also like me. Now I do not see any things with my closed eyes. Do you see any things with your closed eyes? Certainly not. If our eyes are open, we can see everything, if our eyes are closed, we cannot see anything.

Eyes have eyelids, eyebrows, eyeballs. These are your eyebrows, these are your eyelids, and inside your eyes are eyeballs that are round as that of a cat - a pussy cat that comes to our house every now and then.

In this way parents particularly the mothers can teach their children the different words they find in and around them. Simultaneously the children should be acquainted with the meaning of these words in their mother tongue also. This will help them to learn their mother tongue beside English.

Formation of words from two, three, four, five, and six letters is necessary. The teachers and the parents should teach the students how to make words from the different letters.

For instance:

1. CAT, RAT, MAT, BAT, FAT, SAT, HAT... CAN, FAN, MAN, RAN, PAN, VAN,
2. MET, LET, SET, JET, BET, GET, NET, PET, VET...
3. COAT, DOT, GOAT, HOT, LOT, NOT, PLOT, VOTE ...
4. FINE, MINE, NINE, DINE, KITE

OTHER WORDS:

Relation: MOTHER, FATHER, BROTHER, SISTER, UNCLE, AUNT, GRANDFATHER, GRANDMOTHER,

Names of animals: DOG, CAT, COW, BUFFALOW, HORSE, ELEPHANT, DONKEY, LION, TIGER, ZEBRA, BEAR, DEAR, FOX, HARE ...

Names of birds: CROW, CUCKOO, SPARROW, PARROT, KITE, VULTURE, CRANE, DUCK, COCK ...

Names of flowers: ROSE, LILY, LOTUS, SUNFLOWER...

Names of fruits: MANGO, ORANGE, GRAPES, PAPAYA, GUAVA, COCOANUT...

All these things are found in and around us. We can show them to our wards. If they see with their own eyes, they can know and learn quickly.

They should be asked to get by heart these words with spelling. Homework should be given to write these words in their copies. Each word at least three times on four lined copies only.

Within a short period of time children can know and learn many words to write, read and speak. Only the important thing is that the parents at home and teachers in school ought to guide the children so attentively that the children can perform excellently in their classes.

Not only do I hope but believe also that the guidelines duly elucidated and explained above can be very useful for the parents and the teachers in teaching the students jointly for a common cause i.e. excellent performance in examinations/tests.

*   *   *

E – ENGLISH GRAMMAR (SENTENCE ONLY)

Description

E- Grammar in English is a series of all chapters of English Grammar in piecemeal.

A series of "Blue Books" has been published till now on different topics or subjects such as love short stories, travel experience about the historical places, essays, comments, and E – Grammar.

Under E- Grammar Blue Book series 4 books (Orthography, Etymology, Narration and Analysis have already been published in Google Play.

It is the fifth E – Grammar in which all the necessary details about a sentence, its definition, its salient features and characteristics, its comparison to phrase and clause have been explained so logically that students of higher classes can understand very clearly with ease.

The E- Blue Book is not only for the students but for those beginners also who want to learn English language and literature. Most of the English Grammars begin with the primary chapter of "Sentence." Even the eminent grammarian Nesfield has started his world famous grammar with the chapter of sentence.

The book is very useful to all who are interested in learning English.

You can access to Google Play and in Search column type simply Durga Prasad, a list of Blue Books will appear and you can select this book, buy online and can read.

Durga Prasad
Author

*   *   *

Sentence

Mathew: Sir! You have taught us about Orthography and Etymology. We have learnt how methodically and beautifully we should write alphabet – 26 letters from A to Z in capital letters as well as in small letters. We have learnt the art of writing these letters too.

Sir! You have taught us about Etymology also – composing word/words joining one letter to another. We can now form or compose word or words that are meaningful in sense.

Sir! Now we want to learn how to make a sentence.

Teacher: Well! I am happy all of you have followed me and have learnt both the important chapters of grammar. Now I want to teach you about sentence – its definition, its salient feature, its important parts, its kind according to sense and its kind according to its form.

Define a sentence.

Mathew: Sir! A sentence is a group of words.

Teacher: No, it is a group of words that carry sense. Even a single word may be a sentence, and even a group of too many words may not be a sentence.

Mathew: Is it so?

Teacher: Why not? Let us see.

For instance – Go. Do. Play. Dance. Sing. Each word is a sentence as each carries sense or meaning. It appears from each word that somebody is ordering someone to do something. Pronoun "You" is inherent or implied and as such the sentence will be: You go. You do. You play. You dance. You sing. All these sentences are called Imperative Sentences according to meaning wherein somebody requests, prohibits (forbids), orders someone to do a certain piece of work, requests or forbids to do a certain work.

Now see these group of words: He goes. She does. We play. They dance. She sings. Each one is a group of merely two words but each has complete sense.

In each one we find a subject and a finite verb in place of a predicate. So each one is a sentence as having complete sense or meaning.

Hence a sentence is a group of words that carries complete sense.

Let us see some other group of words which are as long as a sentence but they are not sentences as do not make complete sense or meaning.

A) For instances:

1. In spite of difficulties
2. In the long run
3. Early in the morning
4. Having done his duty
5. Once upon a time

These groups of words from serial number 1 to 5 do not make complete sense, as such these are not sentences. They do not have subjects nor finite verbs. They are called phrases.

Teacher: Can anyone define a phrase?

Ruby: Yes, Sir! A group of words that does not make complete sense or meaning.

Such as Mathew going to market lost his purse. Here "going to market" is a phrase since it does not make complete sense.

Teacher: Very good. We see that a phrase has no finite verb nor a subject. We can also say that a group of words without a finite verb, without a subject and without complete sense is a phrase.

In fact a phrase is a meaningless part of a sentence.

In examples 1 to 5 in (A) above are phrases. Now there should not be any confusion between a sentence and a phrase.

Mathew: Sir! Sometimes we are confused about a sentence and about a clause.

Teacher: Don't be confused at all. I have already defined a sentence and its characteristics also.

Now I tell you about a clause.

A group of words that does not make complete sense though it has a finite verb of its own and a subject of its own too.

A clause has some sense but does not have complete sense.

A clause has a finite verb of its own and a subject of its own too.

For instances: The following are the examples of clauses

1. When the thief ran away
2. Where Philips lives at
3. Why Margret cheated me
4. What John said
5. Who loves his fellowmen

From the examples 1 to 5 we find each carries some sense but not complete sense, though each has a finite verb of its own and a subject of its own.

Let us conclude for ever:

1. A sentence has complete sense with its finite verb of own.
2. A phrase has incomplete sense. It has no finite verb of its own.
3. A clause has incomplete sense though it has a finite verb and a subject of its own.

I think now it is very clear to you.

All students: Yes, Sir!

Teacher: Very good.

Have you followed what a sentence is.

Ruby: Yes, Sir! A sentence is a group of words that makes complete sense.

Mathew: Sir! A sentence is a group of words that has complete sense or meaning.

Teacher: OK. I am happy you have followed me. Your definitions are right but something more important characteristics of a sentence you ought to know.

Ruby: Please tell us, Sir!

1. A sentence always starts with a capital letter.
    For instance: Go. Go to school now. Why do you go to school? Who will bell the cat? Where is he going now? When the cat is away, the mice will play. All that glitters in not gold. Unity is strength. He that is down needs fear no fall. Labour never goes in vain. Necessity is the mother of invention. Impossibility is found in fool's dictionary. What a beautiful scene it is! How foolish he is!
    In all the above sentences we find either a full stop, or an interrogative sign or an exclamatory sign.
2. A sentence either ends with a full stop or an interrogative sign or exclamatory sign.
3. A sentence has a subject and a predicate (A combination of a subject and predicate) and the predicate may have different parts of speech and different complements etc. – all these must be in order in order to make a complete sense.

Margret: Can you teach us now?

Teacher: Not now but in the next chapter that will follow one by one as deems fit. Forget it for the time being and concentrate on what I teach you consecutively one by one.

Teacher: There must be a subject in a sentence – subject may be a person, a place or a thing – subject may be a pronoun - subject may be an infinitive "To" (As – To walk is a good exercise.) - Subject may be a gerund noun (AS – Walking is a good exercise.) - Subject may be the finite verb only (As- Go. Sing. Dance. Play.)- Subject may be a subordinate noun clause

Now some examples are given for you to understand clearly:

(A) Subject as a noun

a) Mathew does his homework regularly. – Person
b) India defeated South Africa. – Place
c) An apple fell down from the tree. – Thing

(B)Subject as a pronoun

I play football. We go to school. You can sing this song. He loves his mother. She gets up early in the morning. It rains today. This causes a problem. They obey their parents.

(C) Subject as infinite "To"

To walk is a good exercise. To take meal in time is a good habit. To err is human. To forgive is divine. To break the rule is punishable. To take bribe is a crime.

(D) Subject as a gerund noun

Walking is a good exercise. Taking meal in time is a good habit. Breaking the rule is punishable. Taking bribe is a crime. Smoking is injurious to health. Taking tobacco can cause cancer.

(E) Subject as a finite verb only

Go., Sing., Dance., Play. In all these sentences the subject "You" is inherent or implied. It appears that somebody is ordering someone to do a certain work. When I teach you about the kinds of sentence in next chapter- "Kinds of Sentence" according to meaning, you will know more about it.

(F) Subject as a subordinate noun clause

1. When the thief ran away is not known to me.
2. Where Philips lives at is unknown to his teacher.
3. Why Margret cheated me is unbelievable.
4. What John said is not true.
5. Who loves his fellowmen is loved by God.

In all the cited sentences if you find out the subject, it is neither a noun, nor a pronoun, nor an infinitive 'to' nor a gerund noun, it is a subordinate noun clause. So a subordinate noun clause can be a subject of a sentence. When I teach you Analysis chapter, you will learn it in details.

Do you follow me?

All students: Yes, Sir!

Normally subject precedes its verb – I mean to say subject comes before its finite verb but in some exceptional cases subject comes after its finite verb.

For instance: 1 - There lived a king in Patliputra.

2. Here is your pen that you lost yesterday.

There must be a finite verb followed by its subject.

Subject means who/which does something – subject may be a living one or non -living one.

We can find or trace out the subject by asking a question starting with "Who" or "What".

For instance: Rosy is going to school.

Who is going to school?

Answer is – Rosy. Here rosy is the subject of the sentence.

An apple has fallen down from the tree.

What has fallen down from the tree?

The answer is – An apple. Here an apple is the subject in the sentence.

Teacher: Dear boys and girls you have learnt a lot about a sentence, about a phrase and moreover about a clause and I am confident there is no confusion at all now in knowing each one and the difference from one to other.

Now I want to teach you something more about a subject and about a predicate. These are also necessary to teach you.

1. **Subject: Subject is a word or a group of words who does something or something is done by him or her or by anything else or about whom or about which something is said. Thus a subject is a doer of a work or a thing.**

What will be a subject of a sentence has already been taught to you in the earlier paragraph. It is unnecessary to repeat it again.

Whenever we read about subject in the respective chapter of grammar, we find subject and predicate.

I have already taught you about subject in details. Isn't it?

All students: Yes, Sir! It is not necessary to revise it since we have followed it clearly, and if lagging something, we will revise it in our houses.

Teacher: Very good.

It's very simple to understand.

Whatever is said about the subject is a predicate.

It starts from or begins with the finite verb that follows its subject to the end of the sentence irrespective of how long or how short the sentence is.

For instance:

1. I read my lesson.
2. I read my lesson every day.
3. I read my lesson every day in the morning.
4. I read my lesson every day in the morning with my younger brother, Smith.
5. I read my lesson every day in the morning with my younger brother, Smith who reads in the same school where I read.

    Just notice all the sentences from serial number 1 to 5.

    I have written all these sentences in short as well as in long only to clarify the subject and the predicate.

Now as I told you:

"I" is the subject in all the sentences and the other parts of the sentence after "I" is the predicate irrespective of how short or long it is.

I understand all of you have learnt all important things about a sentence and also about so many important things relevant to it.

All students: Thank you, Sir! We are very happy you have taught us so simply, so nicely with examples or instances.

Teacher: May God guide you in what you learn either in your classes or at your homes!

* * *

E – ENGLISH GRAMMAR (KINDS OF SENTENCE)

Description

"Kind of Sentence" is one of the primary chapters of English Grammar. The earlier E-Books of Orthography (About alphabet) and in Etymology (About word formation) are already published in Google Play for the students who are in learning stage. In another E-Book the author has written about sentence defining it with examples bur in the relevant E-Book "Kind of Sentence" is explained with suitable examples.

In two ways kind of sentence is explained:

1. **According to sense.**
2. **According to form or structure.**

You can access to Google Play and by typing the author's name in search column, the book among more than other 60 books will appear also. You can select and buy it online for reading either in your smartphone or laptop or desktop or tablet with accessibility to internet. The price is Rs.120 only.

The price of the book looks more but its contents are more valuable than the price you pay for it because each kind of sentence is well defined and is explained very clearly and the examples are cited relevantly to make the subject understandable with ease. The author is of the opinion that it is incomparable and it is also unique of its kind.

Durga Prasad
Author

*   *   *

Kinds of Sentences

There are four kinds (types) of sentences according to sense:

A) Assertive Sentence: Assertive Sentence is also called declarative sentence – some statement is declared in affirmation or negation as the case may be in Assertive Sentences.

In Assertive Sentences the statement can be in affirmation of something else or can be in negation of something else

Thus we find two types or kinds of Assertive Sentences:

i) First one is called Affirmative Sentence and
ii) The second one is called Negative Sentence

It will be clear with the examples as follows:

1. Go.
2. You are a student.
3. I have a pen to write with.
4. We should do our duty.
5. He was a great warrior.
6. The old man met me yesterday.
7. Mathew was going to his school.
8. Please give him your pen.
9. Get out of the room.
10. My uncle will come tomorrow.
11. Take rest.
12. We can win the game.
13. They may pay their dues today.

All the above sentences are affirmative sentences as we find that something is said in form of statement and each statement is in the affirmative, as such all are affirmative sentences.

Now let us see the following examples:

1. Do not go.
2. You are not a student.

3.   I have no pen to write with.
4.   We should not tell a lie.
5.   He was not a great warrior.
6.   The old man did not meet me yesterday.
7.   Mathew was not going to school.
8.   Please do not give him your pen.
9.   Do not get out of the room.
10. My uncle will not come tomorrow.
11. Do not take rest unless you finish your job.
12. We cannot win the match.
13. They may not pay their dues today.

We find that in all the sentences cited above are the examples of Negative Sentences as in each statement something is in refusal or denial or in the negation.

"No" and "Not" are the signs of negation and as such "no" or "not" has been used in all the sentences cited above.

The sign of negation No or Not is used normally in full form but may be used in short form also.

am not – amn't, is not – isn't, are not – aren't, was not - wasn't, were not – weren't, have not – haven't, has not – hasn't, had not – hadn't, do not – don't, does not – doesn't, did not – didn't, cannot – can't, could not – couldn't, shall not – shan't, should not – shouldn't, must not – mustn't, will not – won't, would not – wouldn't, need not – needn't, dare not – daren't.

But it is noted that in affirmative sentences only the following are in short forms:

I am – I'm, I have – I've, I shall or I will – I'll and That is – That's.

More about Negative Sentence: Some sentences do not have signs of negation – No or not, even then the sentences carry the negative meaning or sense. In such cases prefixes or suffixes are used before or after the word - prefixes normally before adjectives, nouns, verbs, adverbs etc. and suffixes normally after nouns etc. It will be clear by the following examples:

Some of the prefixes are as follows:

A) Un
B) In
C) Im

D) Ir

E) Dis

F) il

Just see these words:

A) – i) Able, even, wanted, aware, well, willing, accountable, adopted, answerable, balanced, certain, clean, comfortable, common, compromising, conditional, conscious, crowned, deniable, acceptable, ashamed, attended, authorised, avoidable, bearable, breakable, controllable, fit and so on.. – All adjectives.

ii)   Do, bend, bosom, cap, cork, cover, tie, screw and so on... - All verbs. Willingly, commonly, certainly, comfortably, conditionally and so on...- All adverbs.

If the prefix "un" is added before any of the word/words given in (A), the sense in the affirmative is changed into that of the negative one/ones. For instance: unable from able, uneven from even, unwanted from wanted, unaware from aware, unwilling from willing and so on ... Now let us see the sentences in both the senses – Affirmative as well as Negative;

(A)   a) My servant is able to do this work. B) My servant is unable to do this work.

c) My wife is aware of my weaknesses. – d) My wife is unaware of my weaknesses.

e) His arrival is certain. – f) His arrival is uncertain.

If you notice all the above noted three sentences in b, d and f you will not find No or Not but the sentences are in the negative.

A)   –i)- complete, accessible, adequate, advertent, advisable, appropriate, capable, coherent, comparable, competent, congruous, consistent, conspicuous, convenient, correct, corrigible, credible, definite, direct, discipline, divisible, edible, evitable, famous, fertile, flammable, finite, flexible, formal, human, sensitive, solvent, subordinate, sufficient and so on... All adjectives

ii) From adjectives nouns may be made, not necessary to go into details.

iii) From adjectives adverbs may be made, not necessary to explain here further.

Just see some sentences:

1.   a) My job is complete. b) My job is incomplete.
c) The judge is competent to pass this order. d) The judge is incompetent to pass this order.
Again see some words:

a)   from possible to impossible, from practicable to impracticable, probable to improbable, pure to impure,

b)   relevant to irrelevant, responsible to irresponsible, rational to irrational, regular to irregular, repairable to irreparable, resistible to irresistible, respective to irrespective, reversible to irreversible,

c)   from advantageous to disadvantageous, agree to disagree, appear to disappear, appoint to disappoint, approve to disapprove, arm to disarm, believe to disbelieve, claim to disclaim, colour to discolour, comfort to discomfort, courage to discourage, figure to disfigure, honest to dishonest, honour to dishonour, like to dislike, pleasure to displeasure and so on…

d)   legal to illegal, legible to illegible, legitimate to illegitimate, literate to illiterate, logical to illogical and so on…

I want to make it clear that even without use of sign/signs of negation i.e. no or not a sentence may be a negative sentence in sense or meaning.

We can mark these sentences:

It is not legal. We can say it another sentence without using no or not:

It is illegal. It is not legible. – It is illegible. It is not relevant. – It is irrelevant. It is not possible. We can say in another words: It is impossible.

Likewise suffixes can also be used to make the sense of the sentence negative though the sign of negation – no or not is not used in the sentence. For example: Wine is of no use. We can say in another words: Wine is useless. This broken glass is of no worth. We can say it in another way: The broken glass is worthless. In both the sentences "less" suffix is used after the words use and worth. Here also the sense of both the sentences are negative though the sign/signs of negation is not used.

Likewise senseless, careless, harmless, tactless and so on…

I don't feel you have not followed me what I wanted to explain about the affirmative and the negative sentences.

Necessity of learning affirmative and negative sentences arises due to the fact that whenever somebody asks you a question, you will have to reply either in the affirmative sentence or in the negative sentence as the case may be in the right or wrong sense of the term. It will be clear with the following instances:

1. Your friend says to you, "Are you going to school today?"

If you understand as to what your friend wants to know from you, you will have to reply either in the affirmative or in the negative sentence. If you are going to school today, your reply will be as follows:

Yes, I am going to school today.

On the other hand if you are not going to school today, your reply will be as follows:

No, I am not going to school today.

1. Your teacher asks you, "Does the Sun rise in the east?"
2. Your teacher asks you, "Dose the Sun rise in the west?"
3. Your teacher asks you, "Doesn't the Sun rise in the east?"

Against question no. 1 your reply will be in the affirmative:

Yes, the Sun rises in the east.

Against question no. 2 your reply will be in the negative:

No, the Sun doesn't rise in the west.

Against question no. 3 your reply must be in the affirmative Of course, the Sun rises in the east.

Your teacher wants to know something from you by asking a question in interrogative sentences in question nos. 1, 2 and 3. Now you will have to reply either in affirmative sentence or in negative sentence as the case may be.

In view of the reply you make one by one, you must know how to make affirmative sentence and how to make negative sentence to reply the questions correctly. As such in view of the necessity of learning affirmative and negative sentences is a must for those who want to learn English.

I like to revise the chapter once again so that you can follow it and get by heart some examples to quote if required.

1. Assertive Sentence: It is further divided into as follows:

   A) Affirmative Sentence and
   B) Negative Sentence

If we classify sentences afresh, we can know them better by individual name:

1. Affirmative Sentence
2. Negative sentence

It is no wrong if we rename "Affirmative Sentence" as "Positive Sentence," since it carries the same sense or same meaning.

One important thing that puzzles my mind is about the "Interrogative Sentence" and its important role in learning English language and literature.

In my opinion it should precede "Assertive Sentence" in order of priority due to the fact that in most of the houses wherein parents and their children live together, days start with the interrogative sentences and similarly end in interrogative sentences.

How it happens will be clear with the following examples:

1. Phillips! Why do you get up so late?
2. Mathew! Have you taken your breakfast?
3. Ruby! Have you done your homework?
4. Rosy! Why are you crying?
5. Where have you kept your school bag?
6. Do you take tea or coffee?
7. Is it the time to go out of your room?
8. Will you take care of the baby?

I mean to say that interrogative sentences are used more frequently by the parents to know something from their children. As such everyone who desires to learn English must know how to make interrogative sentences.

You cannot know anything from anyone unless or until you get the reply by asking him or her in interrogative sentence. Now comes "Interrogative Sentence."

If we ignore Assertive Sentence and consider Affirmative and Negative sentences of its division into two parts as explained above as 1 and 2, Interrogative Sentence will be 3rd. one so far as the kinds of sentence are concerned. Let us now learn what an interrogative sentence is and its feature.

B) Interrogative Sentences: When anyone askes any question from someone, he or she has to question or makes query in a questionnaire form which is termed as interrogative sentence. In another words we can say that someone interrogates somebody, the sentence or sentences that are used by him or by her is or are interrogative sentences.

There are two important characteristics/ features as to how we can make interrogative sentences and as to how we can identify the interrogative sentences.

1. By placing the auxiliary verb before its subject and
2. By putting a sign of interrogation at the end of the sentence i.e. in place of full stop as done in case of affirmative or negative sentence. It will be clear by the following examples:

    A) You walk in the morning daily. – Present Indefinite Tense
    B) You are walking in the morning daily. Present Imperfect Tense
    C) You have done your homework. – Present Perfect Tense
    D) You have been singing for two hours. – Present Perfect Cont. Tense

In present and past indefinite tense we do not find any auxiliary verb in the sentence.

In present indefinite tense do or does is used as per the number and person of the subject. In all cases do acts as an auxiliary verb save and except in case of singular number and third person. In singular number third person does is used as an auxiliary verb in present indefinite tense.

In past indefinite tense only did is used in all numbers and persons, so here you should not be selective.

So interrogative sentences from 1 to 4 as above will be as follows:

1. Do you walk in the morning daily?
2. Are you walking in the morning daily?
3. Have you done your homework?
4. Have you been singing for two hours?

What I have done in making interrogative sentences may be seen attentively.

1. I have shifted the auxiliary verb from its original place and placed it before its subject.
2. I have put a sign of interrogation at the end of each sentence.

Likewise in past tense and in future tense you can follow the rules and can make interrogative sentence.

Secondly interrogative sentences also begin with interrogative pronouns but the basic rule will remain the same to follow in all cases i.e. the auxiliary verb will precede its subject. For instance:

The following are the interrogative pronouns and the interrogative sentences also begin with them:

a) Where do you live at?
b) Where are you coming from?
c) Where will you settle after retirement?
d) Where is your school bag?
e) When will you come back from Patna?
f) When is your younger brother resuming his duty?
g) When have repaid your loan?
h) When was your sister born?
i) How will you solve this problem?
j) How are you?
k) How have you settled your case?
l) How far is your school from your house?
m) Why are you sad today?
n) Why have you abused me?
o) Why are you begging door to door?
p) Why will she help you?
q) Which book do you like most?
r) Which place does your mother want to visit?
s) Which do you like better – coffee or tea?
t) What is your name?
u) What will be the cost of a van?
v) What can I do for you?

w) What have you decided for filing nomination?

x) Whom do you want to appoint for the post?

All the sentences cited above are interrogative sentences not started with auxiliaries but with interrogative pronouns. But the basic rule i.e. the auxiliary verb precedes its subject in all interrogative sentences remains the same.

At length it will be taught while teaching "Tense" in the subsequent E-Book.

Altogether taking into consideration present and past tenses all auxiliaries are 26 in number which are as follows:

Am, is, are, was, were, be, been, have, has, had, can, could, do, does, did, shall, should, will, would, may, might, must, ought to, need, dare, used to.

One thing I want to make it clear that do, does, did - do not have any meaning -means these are meaningless when they are used as auxiliaries.

There are tag questions also.

1. He is honest, isn't he?
2. She is not honest, is he?
3. You are a teacher, aren't you?
4. You are not a farmer, are you?
5. They can do this work, can't they?
6. She didn't obey me, did she?
7. He won the match, didn't he?

And so on…

Some questions but with long, short and very short answers:

1. Questions: A) Is she your younger sister?
   Answer:

   a) Yes, she is my younger sister. - Long answer.
   b) Yes, she is. - Short answer.
   c) Yes. - Very short answer.

Likewise we can make questions with long, short and very short answers as the case may be. You can learn more about the relevant word/words/subject which could not be explained here in details as deem unnecessary in the present chapter of "Kinds of Sentences. It is very essential to make interrogative sentences if you want to learn English. In our day to day conversation we have to know many things from the people we meet and deal with and in course of our dealing with, we have to ask questions and you can question only when you know how to make questionnaire.

The question of teaching those whose mother tongue is English does not arise at all inasmuch as the babies learn to speak English in the family wherein they are born and brought up. English being mother tongue is not more difficult than those whose mother tongue is not English, rather their mother tongue is a language quite different from them.

In fact the problem is with them whose mother tongue is not English. They have to learn English language at homes and in schools. The children between the age group of three and a half and five can learn English from the very beginning if their schools are of English medium and the children are taught English from nursery classes from A to Z i.e. alphabets.

C) Imperative Sentence: A sentence in which some order or command, request or advice or suggestion or prohibition (Not to do something) is given by someone to somebody.

a) Order or command: Some higher authority or some senior persons order their subordinates or junior ones to obey, such sentences are called imperative sentences. Such sentences begin with finite verbs and the subject "You" is always inherent.

   i) Get out of the class.
   ii) Go and fetch a glass of water.
   iii) Give me your revolver.
   iv) Get down from the tree.
   v) Hang him till death.
   vi) Stand up on the bench.
   vii) Attend your office in time.
   viii) Be punctual. If we see all these sentences, we will find somebody passing order to someone to obey.

"You" is inherent as subject before its finite verb.

b) Request: Here somebody requests someone to do a certain job/work, politeness is there in the statement as if some junior or subordinate says something but politely. Such sentence starts with please or kindly, ends in please or kindly suitably.

    i)   Please open the window.
    ii) Please lend me your book.
    iii) Please allow me to say in my defence.
    iv) Get down from the tree, please.
    v) Kindly show me your identity card.

c) Advice or suggestion: Some advice or suggestion is given by someone to somebody to follow.

    i)   Stand in a queue, your turn will come soon.
    ii) Have patience, you will win the match.
    iii) Early to bed and early to rise makes a man healthy, wealthy and wise.

d) Prohibition (Forbid): Somebody forbids someone to do something. In another word in a simple way we can find someone telling someone not to do a certain piece of work/job. Such sentences always start with "Do not".

    i)   Do not walk in the sun.
    ii) Do not tell a lie.
    iii) Do not disobey your parents.
    iv) Do not spit in public places.
    v) Do not abuse me.
    vi) Do not be late in attending your class.

D) Exclamatory Sentence: Such sentences in which we express our emotion all of a sudden as a sort of surprise (wonder, astonishment), pleasure (delight, happiness), pain, sorrow, grief, anger, desire (wish), repentance, disgust etc. are known as Exclamatory Sentences. Such sentences start normally with – what, how, O that, Alas, Hurrah, Would that, If I, If only, May, and start normally with a single word of adjective only. For instance: Superb!, Wonderful!,

Marvellous!, Fantastic!, Amazing! Etc. Now let us understand it clearly with examples:

a) Wonder: It normally starts with what or how:

  i) What a beautiful scene it is!
  ii) What a beautiful scene! (In short)
  iii) How immensely mother loved her baby!
  iv) How nicely she wrote the answer!

b) Pleasure: It normally starts with some sign as a sort of sudden emotion.

  i) Hurrah, we have won the match!
  ii) Bravo, Australia won the world cup 2015!

c) Sorrow, grief, pain: Starts with Alas

  i) Alas, we have lost the match!

d) Desire (wish): i) If I were a king! ii) O that I were a bird! Iii) Would that I had never lost my patience! iv) May the king live long! v) May God guide you in what you do!

E) Optative Sentence: In which wish, desire or pray is expressed by someone. Normally sentences begin with "May" and after the end of the sentence either full stop or sign of exclamation is used. For example:

a) Wish you a happy conjugal life!
b) May God bless with a baby!
c) Best wishes!
d) May you live long!
e) Wish you a happy birth day.

Since the sign of exclamation is used and wish, desire or pray is expressed in optative sentence, some authors have ignored it as one of the kinds of sentence in their books, they have included in exclamatory sentence. I am sure you have learnt much more about the kinds of sentence and will be able to understand each sentence and will be reply correctly in all occasions or situations you will happen to come across. In another way i.e. according to form or structure there are three kinds of sentence:

1. Simple Sentence
2. Compound Sentence
3. Complex sentence

1: Simple Sentence: Definition: A sentence which has only one finite verb in it is called a Simple Sentence. For example:

A) Monica goes to school.
B) He is an honest man.
C) We will attend the meeting in time.
D) He wrote a letter to his friend.
E) You may go out of the meeting hall.

Each sentence from A to E has only one finite verb as such each one is a simple sentence.

2: Compound Sentence: A Compound Sentence is that in which there is at least a Principal Clause and a Co-ordinate Clause joined with co-ordinating conjunction. Let us understand clause first:

A) A clause is a part of a sentence with its own subject and with its own finite verb and when more than such clauses are joined by coordinating conjunction, the sentence such formed after joining is called a Compound sentence. For example:

a) This is the house where I live in.
b) Do not go unless you finish your job.
c) You called him but he didn't listen to you.

Each one has more than one clauses:
a) I) This is the house – Principal or Main Clause.
II) Where I live in – Subordinate clause.
b) I) Do not go – Principal Clause or Main Clause.
II) Unless you finish your job – Subordinate Clause.

c) I) You called him – Principal Clause or Main Clause.

    II) But he didn't listen to me – Coordinating Clause.

3. Complex Sentence: Definition: Complex sentence is a sentence which is made up of at least one Principal or Main Clause and at least one or more Subordinate Clauses – either Subordinate Noun Clause or Subordinate Adjective Clause or Subordinate Adverb Clause. For example:

a) I do not know where he lives at.
b) When he will arrive is not known to me.
c) The house where I live in is not ventilated.
d) The book which I like most is the Geeta.
e) He that is down needs fear no fall.
f) All that glitters is not gold.
g) I will not come if it rains.

All the sentences from a) to g) are complex sentences as there are one Principal Clause and one Subordinate Clause.

Do hope you have followed me while teaching "Kinds of Sentence" as par the sense and as par the form or structure of sentence.

*   *   *

E – ENGLISH GRAMMAR (PARTS OF SPEECH)

Description

"Parts of Speech" is one of the most important chapters of English Grammar.

The author has been an experienced teacher of English language and literature.

After thorough study of English Grammars, he has got a very good knowledge of each and every important chapter. His idea of writing E-Grammar chapter wise is to make it available selectively as a sort of a short story any time on Smartphone, Laptop, Desktop, Tablet etc. with internet connectivity.

He has written this important chapter in a very logical manner explaining each part of speech with suitable examples so that the students can grasp easily and can learn it properly.

What the author has presented is a unique one and any one can find it quite different from so many chapters of Parts of Speech.

You can access to Google Play and after typing the author's name in search column, you can read it as advised to pay Rs.120 only online. The price of E-Book containing a few pages may look more but every part of speech is well defined in a very simple language, explained clearly and the examples are cited relevantly to make the subject understandable with ease. In author's opinion it is incomparable and unique of its kind.

Durga Prasad
Author

* * *

PARTS OF SPEECH

Parts of Speech is an important chapter of English Grammar and this chapter includes all the words that we come across in our day to day life while listening to anything or writing anything or reading anything or moreover speaking anything in English language and literature. The words that we use in any way, in any purpose are termed as "Parts Of Speech."

They are the vital parts that facilitate in learning English language.

The Parts Of Speech are of 8 kinds as follows:

1. Noun
2. Pronoun
3. Adjective
4. Verb
5. Adverb
6. Preposition
7. Conjunction
8. Interjection

As per the modern methodology of grammar that is taught these days to student is again classified into two parts:

1. The form or structure of the words that tend to change in its usage.
2. The form or structure of words that do not tend to change, they remain the same in its usage.

In the first category the parts of speech that come are as follows:

1. Noun
2. Adjective
3. Verb
4. Adverb

In the second category the parts of speech that come are as follows:

1. Pronoun
2. Preposition

3. Conjunction
4. Interjection

1. Noun: Definition:

A) Noun is a naming word. For instance – Johnson, Smith, Phillips, London, America, India, The Bible, The Ganges, The Sun.

B) Noun is a name of a person, place or thing. For example – Rohit Sharma, Sachin Tendulkar, Bill Gates, Mukesh Ambani, Ratan Tata, Mumbai, New York, Tokyo, Sydney, Berlin, Paris, Shanghai, apple, bat, cat, dog, elephant etc.

Kinds Of Noun: Noun is of five kinds:

1. Proper Noun
2. Common Noun
3. Material Noun
4. Collective Noun
5. Abstract Noun

1. Proper Noun: Proper Noun is the name of a proper person or a proper place or a proper thing. Proper Noun has got a particular identity, a particular recognition and we know or call them by his/her/its name.

A) Person: Mahatma Gandhi, Jesus Christ, Alfred Nobel, John Milton, Pablo Neruda, Bertrand Russell, Abraham Lincoln, Martin Luther, Swami Vivekanand, Margret Thatcher and so on…

B) Place: New Delhi, Kolkata, Washington, China, Russia, Japan, New Zealand, South Africa, India, Pakistan, Sri Lanka, England, Australia, West Indies and so on…

C) Thing: The Geeta, The Koran, The Bible, The Sun, The Moon, Cow, dog, water, milk, gold, silver, army, class, jury, beauty, character, unity, wisdom, Hinduism, Buddhism, Christianity, religion, education, childhood, cleverness and so on…

2. Common Noun: Such a word which denotes its whole such persons or whole animals, birds, beasts, whole things. It indicates a class or a

group with a single word and as such it is termed as common noun. For example:

A) Man: Man is mortal. It means the whole community or class or group of men/ woman are mortal and one day earlier or later will die.
B) Boy, cow, dog, cat: Cow is a four footed animal.
C) Book, pen, paper, pencil: Book is more useful than money.

3. Material Noun: Material Noun is the name/names of such matter, things (quantity) which can be weighed or measured in units of weights or measures. It cannot be counted as number. It is uncountable noun also.

A) Liquid: water, oil, milk, ink: Water is as essential as food. We drink milk daily.
B) Solid: gold, silver, iron, zinc, cotton, wood: Iron is heavier than cotton.
C) Grains: rice, wheat, pulse, sugar, salt: We take rice every day. We mix sugar in our tea.

4. Collective Noun: It indicates a group or collection of persons or things. For example:
Jury: Jury are divided in their opinion.
Team: Indian team was defeated in cricket match.
Army: Indian army are very strong.
Likewise – bunch, flock, union, committee, herd, group, class and so on...

5. Abstract Noun: It indicates only the quality or state of a thing – thing that is abstract, no physical existence, cannot be seen, cannot be touched, cannot be hold of, it has no shape or size or form. In one word we can say that it can be realised or felt only.
As such it is uncountable (not countable).

A): Quality/feature/character: Honesty is the best policy. Here honesty and policy are abstract nouns. Charity begins at home. Here charity is an abstract noun. Sympathy is far better than gold. Here sympathy is an abstract noun. Man is the master of his own destiny. Here destiny is an abstract noun. Necessity is the mother of invention. Here necessity and invention are the abstract nouns.

Note: It will be dealt with in details separately in a separate E-Blue Book on Noun only.

2. Pronoun: Definition:

1. Pronoun is a replacing word of noun.
2. The word which is used in place of noun is known as pronoun. There is a sound reason for its use in place of noun. If we write an essay or a paragraph and if we repeat the name again and again, it will be inappropriate in writing and in speaking the same name repeatedly. It will be bitter to our mind or heart or our tongue. That is why our great grammarians in the past felt the necessity of a few words that can replace noun and such words that replace noun are termed or known as pronoun. For instance:

A) Mahatma Gandhi was born on 2nd. October 1879. Mahatma Gandhi was born at Porbandar in Gujrat. Mahatma Gandhi was a great patriot. Mahatma Gandhi was a barrister. Mahatma Gandhi fought for freedom of India. Mahatma Gandhi believed in truth and non-violence.

If we see all the sentences written above about Mahatma Gandhi, no sentence is wrong, but the use of Mahatma Gandhi again and again looks odd and inappropriate to our ears and mind. If we use he in place of Mahatma Gandhi in subsequent sentences, it will be appropriate to our ears and mind.

Kinds Of Pronoun: Pronoun is of 10 kinds:

1. Personal Pronoun: Which is used in place of a person, a place or a thing.

    a) I, me, mine – 1st person singular number.
    b) We, us, ours -, plural number
    c) You, yours – 2nd. Person singular & plural number
    d) He, him, his 3rd. person singular number(Masculine)

e) She, her, hers,,,,,, (Faminine)

f) They, them, theirs 3rd. person plural number

g) It – singular neuter gender

2. Possessive Pronoun: Which is used to express possession is called possessive pronoun. For example: mine, ours, yours, his, hers and theirs.

3. Reciprocal: Which is used for reciprocal relationship. For example: one another, each other.

4. Reflexive Pronoun: Which reflexes as the receiver of an action is called reflexive pronoun. For example: myself, ourselves, yourself, himself, herself, themselves, itself.

5. Demonstrative Pronoun: Which is used to demonstrate a person/persons or a thing/things is called demonstrative pronoun. For example: This, that, these, those.

6. Interrogative Pronoun: Which is used to ask question or to make query is called interrogative pronoun. For example: where, when, which, who, what, whom, whose.

   Note: Interrogative sentences also begin with interrogative pronoun but the rule remains the same, that is auxiliary verb precedes its subject. It has been explained in details in another E-Blue Book titled as "Kinds Of Sentence."

7. Relative Pronoun: Which is relative to its noun or pronoun is called relative pronoun. For example: He that is down needs fear no fall. All that glitters is not gold. God helps those who help themselves. In these sentences that and who are the relative pronouns.

8. Indefinite Pronoun: Which does not refer to a definite person, place or a thing. For example: No one or none or nobody, Someone or somebody, Anyone or anybody, anything, anyone

9. Emphasising Pronoun: It is as good as reflexive pronoun. Not necessary to explain it further.

10. Distributive Pronoun: Which refers to a single person or a single thing. For example: Each student was given a prize. Every member is requested to attend the meeting. Either you or your brother can do it. Neither she nor her mother knows how to drive a car. Here each, every, either, neither are the examples of distributive pronoun.

3. Adjective:

The word which qualifies noun or pronoun is called adjective. For example:

A) Alexander was a great warrior.
B) Bhagat Singh was a true patriot.
C) Indian cricket team won the world cup.
D) My children like Chinese food.
E) Can you lend me some money?
F) Do you want any help from me?
G) Eleven players play in a cricket team.
H) We need two workmen to complete this job.
I) This lane is very neat and clean.
J) That city is thickly populated.
K) My factory is just beside the main road.
L) Are you coming from your house?
M) Whose book is this?
N) What time is your father reaching home?
O) I washed my car with my own hands.
P) This is the very place where I was born.

Kinds of Adjective: There are 8 kinds of Adjective:

1. Descriptive Adjective: Example A & B
2. Proper Adjective: Example C & D
3. Quantitative Adjective: Example: E & F
4. Numerical Adjective: Example: G & H
5. Demonstrative adjective: Example: I & J
6. Possessive Adjective: Example: K & L
7. Interrogative Adjective: Example: M & N
8. Emphatic Adjective: Example: O & P

4. Verb: Definition:

1) Verb is a doing word.
2) It is a word that says something about a person or a thing.

3) It is a word showing some act or work or job that is done or performed by someone or by something.

4) It is a word that is used but does not show an action. It is used because it is an important part of a sentence as a subject in a sentence.

5. It is a word that shows a state of mind/ mood or possession of a person or thing.

For example:

a) I cut a tree with an axe.
b) An apple fell down from the tree.
c) My house was repaired this year.
d) I sold my car.
e) I know him personally.
f) I can recognise the culprit.
g) My teacher is unhappy.
h) The sky is clear.
i) I have two hands to work with.
j) She has a big house.

a) b), c) and d) show action, e) and f) do not show any action, g) and h) show state and i) and j) show possession.

Kinds of Verb: There are different categories of division of verb which are as follows:

1.

A) Principal Verb
B) Auxiliary Verb

2.

A) Transitive Verb
B) Intransitive Verb

3.

   A) Finite Verb
   B) Non-finite Verb

1. Principal or Main Verbs are the main verbs that show some action or work or job that is done. Such as eat, drink, sleep, cry, sing, laugh etc.
2. Auxiliary Verb: It is also known as Auxiliaries. It is again divided into three different parts:

A) Primary auxiliaries: be, is, am, are, was, were, have, has, had, do, does – when it is followed by principal verb, it is an auxiliary verb and when it is not followed by the principal verb, it is the main/principal verb. For Example:

1. My son is drinking milk.
2. My son is a student of class three.

In 1. "is" is an auxiliary verb. In 2. "is" is a principal verb.

B. Modal Auxiliaries: the verbs which are used before the principal verbs are Modal auxiliaries verbs. They are: can, could, may, might, will, would, shall, should, must and ought to.

Modal Verbs play a vital role in composition of sentences and vary in its usage also, as such it will be explained in details in another chapter of "Modals" only.

C. Semi-Modal Verbs: They function partly as main and partly as auxiliary verb. For example: need, dare and used to - are such type of verbs. 1. He need not go there. 2. He dare not go there. 3. He used to see me every day.

2.

   A) Transitive Verb: A verb that has its object to make a complete sense. For example: He killed a tiger. I ate an apple. She drank milk.
   B) Intransitive Verb: A verb that has no object of its own, but makes a complete sense. For example: The train stopped all of a sudden. The glass broke into pieces when it fell down from the table.

3.

A) Finite Verb: Finite Verb is such a verb which changes with the change in number and person of its subject. For example:

a) He teaches me English.
b) They teach me English.
c) My mother loves me.
d) We love my mother.

From a to d we find that the verb "Teach" and "Love" change with the change in number and person of its object, so love is a finite Verb.

B. Non-finite Verb: Non-Finite Verb is such a verb which does not change with the change in number and person of its subject, rather it remains the same. For example:

a) My father is going to market to buy a laptop.
b) We are reading books to learn something.
c) They are to obey my order.

Here "to learn" and to "obey" are non-infinite verbs.
Again Non-finite verbs are of three kinds:

a) Infinitive (to+main verb) = To walk is a good execise.
b) Gerund (Main verb + ing) Walking is a good execise.
c) Participle (Main verb + ing, Having + past participle of the main verb) For Example.—a) Going to market he bought a laptop. B) Having finished his duty he left for his house.

Note: verb is as important as subject in a sentence. It will be explained in details separately in an exclusive E-Book.

5.

Adverb: Definition: An adverb is a word which modifies a verb or an adverb or an adjective or so on… in a sentence.

a) My eldest son runs fast.
b) My youngest son runs very fast.
c) My daughter lives in a very beautiful house.

Kinds of adverb:

a) Adverb of time
b)   ,,   of place
c)   ,,   of manner
d)   ,,   of condition
e)   ,,   of degree
f)   ,,   of frequency
g)   ,,   of affirmation or negation
h) Relative adverb
i) Interrogative adverb

6.

Preposition: A preposition is a word which shows relation in between a noun to another noun or a pronoun to another pronoun or noun and so on.

Preposition is a very tough subject. It requires proper attention to learn it thoroughly.

Some of the examples are given below:

a) I live at Pune in India.
b) I get up at 7 o'clock in the morning.
c) My brother is going to school.
d) Rahul is in politics.
e) The book is on the table.
f) I bought a pen to write with.
g) I will come after bath.
h) Are you against my order?

i) My gardener is at work.
j) Please come after 7 o'clock.
k) Please come before 7 o'clock.
l) These dresses are for your children.
m) I am coming from my office.
n) I must obey you, since you are senior to me.
o) The sky is above our head.
p) The cat is under the table.
q) The boy fell into the well.
r) It is within my power.
s) The grapes are beyond my reach.

There are more prepositions which cannot be possible to explain here.
Preposition is mainly of three kinds:

A) Simple: so simple in one word only, for instance at, on, up, in, out, down etc.
B) Compound: It is joined from one simple preposition to another, such as Into, within, beside, without etc.
C) Phrasal preposition: It is used with some other words and makes a phrase, e.g. in front of, on account of, by dint of, because of, in the long run, in lieu of, for want of and so on.
   All such phrase have got a definite sense or meaning and always used invariably in a sentence. The usage of such phrases makes the language and literature ornamental.

6.

Conjunction: Definition: A conjunction is a word which is mainly used for joining words, phrases, clauses or sentences. For example:

A) Dog and cat are pet animals.
B) I like tea and coffee.
C) C.P. Philips as well as his brothers was present in the meeting.
D) Neither I nor my brothers are guilty.
E) Either you or your servant must be punished for abusing me.
F) Mathew is rich but John is poor.

G) Monica may go wherever she likes.
H) Walk carefully lest you should stumble.
I) I will not go out if it rains.
J) Do not leave unless you finish your work.
K) Cotton is not as heavy as iron.
L) All is well that ends well.
M) All that glitters is not gold.
N) The mice will play when the cat is away.
O) He that is down needs fear no fall.

From the above cited examples you have followed what conjunction is and how it functions in a sentence.

Kinds of Conjunction:

A) Coordinating Conjunction: It joins two word or two sentences. For example:

a) Philips and Mathew are my friends.
b) You may take tea or coffee.
c) He is rich but his brother is poor.
d) Mohan as well his brother was present in the meeting.
e) He cannot afford money for he is poor.

B) Correlative Conjunction: It shows correlation in joining words or sentences. For Example:

a) Either he or his brother has stolen my pen.
b) Neither you nor your brother is guilty.
c) He is not only honest but faithful also.
d) Cotton is not heavy as iron is.

C) Subordinating Conjunction: Which joins two or more clauses in a sentence are Subordinating Conjunction. For example:

a) I will lend you money if you pay me interest.
b) You will have to earn your bread as long as you live.
c) Where there is a will, there is a way.

d) No sooner I reached the station than the train had left.

e) You cannot succeed unless you work hard.

f) I do not know why he is sad today.

There are many conjunctions and are used in our day to day life.

8.

Interjection: Definition: An Interjection is a word which is used in expressing sudden feeing of heart or mind when something happens unusual. For example:

a) Alas! We have lost the match! (expressing grief or sorrow)

b) Hurrah! We have won the match! (expressing pleasure or happiness)

c) Bravo! Australia won the final match! (expressing appreciation or praise)

d) Hello! You came in time! (to greet someone)

e) What a dangerous snake! (expressing surprise or wonder)

f) Oh! I am ruined! (expressing sadness or sorrow)

g) Ah! Something has pinched me! (expressing grief or pain)

Dear students! I am sure you have learnt a lot about "Parts of Speech" and will be in a position to use it effectively in your study.

* * *

E – ENGLISH GRAMMAR (ANALYSIS OF SENTENCE ONLY)

Description

Analysis of Sentence is one of the most important chapters of English Grammar.

As English is considered to be an international language, everyone has to learn English language and literature and it can be possible only he/she knows how to write simple sentence, compound sentence, mixed sentence and over and above complex sentence. Moreover it is necessary to know their definitions, their features and the methods of analysing them.

The language of explanation is so simple that even the students of junior classes can understand and grasp easily. It is very useful not for students only but very useful for those also who want to learn good English.

Durga Prasad
Author

*   *   *

Analysis of Sentence

What we feel or think about, we express it in some language. Normally it is expressed in our mother tongue that is taught either at home by the parents or by other family members or by school teachers or so on by the society.

At the infant age of the baby the mother teaches only a few words traditionally for water, milk, head, mouth, ear, eyes, hands, legs, papa, mama, cow, dog, cat, bird, hot, cold, table, chair, book, copy, pen, pencil etc. but with the pace of time the baby grows day by day and parents admit their children in school for primary education. Here the children are taught how to write, read and speak the alphabets, words formation and lastly making sentences.

Keeping in view from the period of infant age, childhood and grown - up age, we find three stages of learning process of languages – the languages that vary from state to state, region to region irrespective of cast, creed, blood, culture, tradition or religion.

We can summarize the period of age in two groups only:

1. Minor Age (3-5 to 10 years aprox.)
2. Major Age (11 to 18 years aprox.)

Again we can divide it taking into consideration the different ages for school going children from nursery to class V – age between about 3.5 years to 10 years. After that 11 to 18 years up to class XII.

In junior classes from nursery to V students learn formation of simple words and simple sentences

From nursery to KG I and KG II students are asked to write names of five animals, five birds, five vegetables, five flowers, this is a cat., that is a dog. etc. Students are asked to recite some nursery rhymes like – "Twinkle, twinkle little stars, how I wonder what you are, "Ba - Ba black ship, have you any wool, yes Sir, yes Sir three bags full." and so on.

Till now question of teaching analysis of sentence does not arise as it is not in their syllabus nor is it required to teach them at their early age.

In senior classes starting from class VI to XII students have to write long answers of the questions asked in the classs or in the examination halls.

Now some portions of grammar are prescribed for each class from VI to XII. The higher the senior classes, the higher the portions of grammar in the syllabus. Now students have to know how to write larger sentences in more than a paragraph.

Earlier in E-Blue Books Series some of the important chapters of English Grammar are already published in "Google Play." Anyone can access to know about the author and about the subject as described, free of cost but to access to the portion of grammar or any article/story one has pay Rs.20 only online. One has to search by typing Durga Prasad or Shubham Kumar in search column, about 6 E-Blue Books or so may appear and to see you will have to click "More Books" eventually all the E-Blue Books in blue colour will start appearing in a series of 6. In all 83 E- Blue Books will appear in a series of six books one by one.

A few are noted below for reference those already published in Google Play:

1. Orthography
2. Etymology
3. Sentence
4. Kinds of Sentence
5. Narration
6. Analysis
7. Parts Of Speech

Now analysis of sentence is explained elaborately so that students can understand the subject thoroughly.

Analysis is one of the most important chapters of English grammar.

Before I teach analysis of sentence, I want to repeat some important features of sentence.

1. What is a sentence?
   Sentence is a group of words that makes complete sense.
2. What are the essential parts of a sentence?
   Subject and predicate: subject is the doer whereas the predicate is its verb only or/and with its object with complements or without complements as the structure or composition of the sentence will be. Let us understand with the examples as follows:

   a) Mathew eats.
   b) Mathew eats bread.

c) Mathew eats bread with his brother.
d) Mathew, my eldest son, eats bread with his brother in the morning.
e) Subject is Mathew and eats is a verb – both make complete sense.
f) Mathew is a subject, eats is a verb and bread is an object.
g) Mathew is a subject, eats is a verb, and with his brother is a complement or extension.
h) Mathew is a subject, eats is a verb, bread is an object and with his brother in the morning is a complement or extension.

All sentences are simple sentences as it has a subject, a transitive verb from a to b and from c to d with complement or extension.

Now I want to explain the chapter as stated above one by one in a simple way:

What does analysis mean in English Grammar?

Analysis means to analyse the sentence in different parts or clauses. As we analyse sentence, it is necessary to know the kinds of sentence as per form. As such I will go by it only and throw light upon it one by one so that any student can follow and grasp quickly.

Kinds of sentence according to form are divided into as follows:

1. Simple Sentence
2. Compound Sentence
3. Mixed Sentence
4. Complex Sentence

Analysis of simple sentence

Simple Sentence is that which has one and only one finite verb preceded by its subject and/or succeeded by its object or/and its complement. For instance:

1. Analysis of Simple Sentence:
   Simple sentence is that in which there is a subject and a finite verb with complete sense. For instance:

1. John writes.
2. Mathew writes a letter.
3. He is a good student.
4. You are a very clever person.

5. We have a beautiful garden.
6. Mr. Shah is the principal of our school.
7. Rama, the son of king Dasrath, killed Ravana, the king of Lanka. Let us analyse these sentences. One can analyse a sentence in many ways but a simple sentence can be analysed in two ways:

1. A simple sentence has some parts as explained below:

These parts into four parts are as follows:

A) Subject
B) Predicate
C) Extension of the subject
D) Extension of the object

John, Mathew, he, you, we, Mr. Shah and Rama are the subjects and the rest of the parts of the sentences are predicate.

Moreover we can analyse further as follows:

My brother, a student of class X, a teacher, the nib of this are also parts of the sentences and they are known as extension of their subjects whereas a letter, a good student, a very clever person, a beautiful garden, the principal of our school, in class ten, ninety percent marks, his students and gold are called the extension of their objects.

We can analyse the simple sentences in another way also:

1. He reads. = He is a subject and reads is a verb.
2. My brother reads his lesson regularly. = My is an attributive, brother is a subject, reads is a verb, his is an attributive (relative pronoun also), regularly is an adverb.
3. He has given a book to me. = He is a subject, has is an auxiliary verb, given is a principal verb, a is an article, book is a direct object, to is a preposition and me is an indirect object.
4. The captain runs very fast. = The is a definite article, captain is a subject, runs is a verb, very is an adverb, fast is also an adverb as "Adverb is a word that qualifies/modifies its preceding verb or adverb.
5. The cow of Gopal gives milk daily. = The cow is a subject, gives is a verb, milk is an object and daily is an adverb.

Note = attributives are adjectives or adjectives equivalents qualifying the subject.

2. Analysis of Compound Sentence

First of all we should define compound sentence.

Compound Sentence is that in which there is at least a Principal Clause and a Co-ordinate Clause joined with co-ordinating conjunction. There may be more than one Principal Clause and Co- ordinate Clause. In Compound Sentence all clauses are supposed to be independent. The principal or main clause is supposed to be Principal Clause and the others beginning with co-ordinating conjunctions are supposed to be Co- ordinate Clause. Co-ordinate Clause always begin with Co- ordinating conjunction i.e. and, but, or, nor, still, yet etc.

For instance:

1. I am a teacher and you are a student.

    A) I am a teacher. – Principal Clause.
    B) You are my student. – Co-ordinate Clause connective – and.

Hence it is a compound sentence.

2. I am poor but you are rich.

    A) I am poor. – Principal Clause.
    B) But you are rich. – Co-ordinate Clause, connective but.

Hence it is a compound sentence.

3. Either John or Mathew will lead the cricket team.

    A) Either John will lead the cricket team – Principal Clause.
    B) Or Mathew will lead the cricket team. – Co- ordinate Clause connective either … or.

Hence it is a compound sentence.

4. Walk carefully otherwise you will fall down.

    A) Walk carefully. - Principal Clause.
    B) Otherwise you will fall down. – Co-ordinate Clause connective otherwise.

3. Analysis of Mixed Sentence

Mixed Sentence is that in which we find all types of clauses i.e. principal clause. Subordinate clause and co- ordinate clause.

1. In mixed sentence you have to analyse and separate all clauses and to name each one with its function.
   Let us make it clear with some suitable examples:

A) He who knows not and knows that he knows not is a fool.

    a) He is a fool. – Principal Clause.
    b) Who knows not – Subordinate Adjective Clause qualifying the pronoun "He" in "A"
    c) And he knows – Co- ordinate Clause – connective and.
    d) That he knows not – Subordinate Noun Clause object to the verb "Knows" in "A".
    Connectives – who, and, that

It is a Mixed Sentence having all types of clauses.
Analysis of Complex Sentence
A complex sentence is that in which there is at least one principal clause and one or more than one subordinate clauses.

To understand complex sentence we should know or define the word "Clause."

A) Clause is a part of a larger sentence which has its own subject and own verb but with incomplete sense. Moreover its sense depends upon the principal clause of the complex sentence.

For instance:

a) When the cat is away, the mice will play.
b) Where there is a will, there is a way.
c) All that glitters is not gold.
d) God helps those who help themselves.
e) Where John lives is not known to me.
f) I do not know what Mathew has said.

When the cat is away, where there is a will, that glitters, who help themselves, where John lives, what Mathew has said – all are clauses since they have their own subjects and own verbs but with incomplete sense. We cannot say that they are sentences since they do not have complete sense or complete meaning. Moreover something remains to know when we read any of the clauses as referred above. We can say all these clauses are subordinate (dependent) to the principal clauses i.e. if we read the principal clause along with the subordinate clause, we get the complete sense or meaning and that is why it is termed as sentence and the sentence is a complex one as it has at least one principal clause and at least one subordinate clause having their own subject and predicate (own finite verbs and objects)

Sometimes the principal clause has no subject as noun or pronoun and it so happens when the subordinate clause is itself the subject of the complex sentence. At the same time if I say it has no subject, it is wrong to say, there is a subject but it is inherent. We have to apply our mind where the subject is inherent and what it is as subject. We cannot imagine even a sentence without a subject as noun or pronoun.

A few instances are given below to understand how subject is inherent and where it is and what it is:

A) Where Mathew lives is not known to me.
B) What you say is not true.
C) When he will arrive in the meeting is not certain.
D) How she has committed suicide is a mystery.
E) Why he has resigned from service is not known to us.

In all above clauses we do not find any subject in the principal clauses, but when we analyse the complex sentences one by one, we find "It" as subject.

Now I analyse them one by one:

A) 1: Where Mathew lives - Subordinate Noun Clause subject to the verb "is"

: It (here it is inherent as subject in the form of pronoun) is not known to me. – Principal Clause.

Similarly in all the principal clauses from B) to E) pronoun "it" as subject is inherent. We can analyse all these complex sentences in the similar way as shown in A) above.

Normally in all principal clauses we notice the subject clearly as noun or pronoun.

It is one part of the complex sentence, another part is related to subordinate (dependant) clause.

Subordinate Clause:

It is always subordinate to the principal clause of the complex sentence. Its sense or meaning is always dependant on that of the principal clause.

To find out the subordinate clause in a complex sentence is not as easy as to find out principal clause but even then we can find it out if we learn the rules and apply our mind to search it.

We can find out subordinate clause and name it whether it is subordinate noun clause and how it is noun clause we can explain with reason.

1. Subordinate Clause begins with subordinating conjunction like when, where, how, why, which, what, what, whom, as, if, whether, because, unless, until, since, for, though, although, lest, otherwise, either, neither, or and so on.
2. Subordinate Clause carries sense but not complete sense though it has its own subject, verb and object and sometimes complement to subject or object.

If anyone wants to learn English language and literature, it is a must to learn analysis of simple sentence, compound sentence, mixed sentence and over and above complex sentence.

Subordinate Clause is of three kinds:

1. Subordinate Noun Clause
2. Subordinate Adjective Clause
3. Subordinate Adverb Clause

1. Subordinate Noun Clause: Let us know the function of noun in a sentence. Noun functions as subject as noun i.e. the naming word of person, place or thing or pronoun used in place of person, place or thing. Such clause begins with subordinating conjunction as explained above.

It would be clear if we examine a complex sentence having a principal clause and a subordinate noun clause subject to the verb of a principal clause:

What the accused said is not true.

Where he lives is not known to me.

When the president will arrive is not scheduled.

Why she is sad is not known to me.

In the subordinate clauses we find that:

A) What the accused said is subject in the complex sentence as such it is Subordinate Noun Clause subject to the verb "is" of the principal clause.
B) Where he lives is subject in the complex sentence as such it is subordinate noun clause subject to the verb "is" of the principal clause.
C) When the president will arrive and why she is sad are also subjects in the complex sentences and as such they are also subordinate noun clauses subject to the verbs "is" in the principal clauses as cited above.

2. Object to the verb: if any subordinate clause functions as object in complex sentence and also begins with subordinating conjunction, it is subordinate noun clause object to the verb of the principal clause of the complex sentence.

For instance:

1. I do not know where John lives at.
2. I did not hear what the accused said.
3. I don't know why your wife is sad.

4. We can ensure when he will attend the court.
5. We do not know how the magician disappears from the stage.

If we analyse principal clause and subordinate clause from the complex sentences we find as follows:

1. I do not know – PC and where John lives at is a subordinate clause and as the subordinate clause functions as object, it is subordinate noun clause object to the verb "know" in the principal clause.
2. Similarly I did not know – PC and what the accused said is subordinate noun clause object to the verb "hear" in the PC.
3. I don't know – PC and why your wife is said is subordinate noun clause object to the verb "know" in the PC.
4. We can ensure – PC and when he will attend the court is subordinate noun clause object to the verb "ensure" in the PC.
5. We do not know – PC and how the magician disappears from the stage is subordinate noun clause object to the verb "know" in the PC.

3. Object to the preposition

Here we find a preposition just before the subordinating conjunction which the subordinate clause starts with. For instance:

1. Your success depends upon how you work.
2. We do not believe in what the accused says.
3. Restart from where you have failed.
   In all these complex sentences we notice some prepositions after which subordinate clause begins with, e.g. how you work after "upon", what the accused says after "in" and where you have failed after "from" as such all such subordinate clauses come under the purview of the rule i.e. object to the preposition and hence all are subordinate noun clauses.

4. In apposition to noun or pronoun

When subordinate clause is in apposition to a noun or a pronoun of the principal clause of the complex sentence, such a subordinate clause becomes subordinate noun clause.

Normally in such cases the subordinate clause begins with co-ordinating conjunction "that". Let us understand it with some examples:

1. The news that the robber was shot dead is true.
2. It is a matter of great pleasure that the principal of our school has hoisted the national flag.
3. The information that all the offices will remain closed on the day of general election is notified for all concerned.
4. It is true that honesty is the best policy.
5. It is a fact that the earth goes round the Sun.

We find from serial nos. 1 to 5 that subordinate clauses begin with "that" are in apposition to some nouns or pronouns viz. news, pleasure, information, it and fact.

We can analyse the complex sentences as follows:

1. The news is true – PC and that the robber was shot dead is subordinate noun clause in apposition to noun "the news" in PC.
2. Likewise from serial 2 to 5 it is a matter of great pleasure, the information is notified for all concerned, it is true and it is a fact – all are principal clauses and
3. Likewise the same "That the principal of our school has hoisted the national flag, that all the offices will remain closed on the day of general election, that honesty is the best policy and that the earth goes round the Sun." – all are subordinate noun clauses in apposition to some nouns, pronouns in the principal clauses of the complex sentences concerned.

Complement to the verb

When a subordinate clause is complement to the verb of the principal clause of the complex sentence or functions as a complement to the verb, such subordinate clause is subordinate noun clause complement to the verb of the principal clause.

For instance:

1. It appears that it will rain for a few days.
2. It seems he will resign soon. (that is inherent)
3. It is certain Virat Kohli will lead the Indian Cricket Team this time. (that is inherent)

Subordinate Adjective Clause

The function of subordinate adjective clause is the same what we find any adjective qualifying its noun or pronoun. As usual the subordinate clause begins with its subordinating conjunction. The conjunction succeeds its noun or pronoun. Sometimes the conjunction does not appear, it is inherent. We should understand what conjunction is inherent by way of qualifying suitably its noun or pronoun. For instance:

1. The books which you buy must be useful.
2. The city where my parents live in is Jaipur, the capital of Rajasthan.
3. The house we live in is far away from our office.
4. The boy whom I like most is a sportsman.
5. The time when you get up from your bed should be noted down.
6. The place where you work should be neat and clean in all respect.

Let us analyse the complex sentence containing subordinate adjective clause and principal clause.

1. The books must be useful. – PC and which you buy – is subordinate adjective clause qualifying the noun "The books" in PC.
2. The city is Jaipur, the capital of Rajasthan. – PC and where my parents live in – Subordinate Adjective Clause qualifying the noun "The city" in the PC.
3. The house is far away from our office. – PC and (where is inherent here) we live in – Subordinate Adjective Clause qualifying the noun "The house" in PC.
4. The boy is a sportsman. – PC and whom I like most – subordinate adjective clause qualifying the noun "The boy" in PC.

5. The time should be noted down. – PC and when you get up from your bed – Subordinate Adjective Clause qualifying the noun the "time" in PC.

6. The place should be neat and clean in all respect.- PC and where you work – Subordinate Adjective Clause qualifying the noun place in PC

4. Subordinate Adverb Clause

The clause which functions as an adverb is an adverb clause. The function of adverb is divided into nine parts:

The other features of subordinate clause remain the same. For example it starts with some subordinating conjunctions. There is peculiarity in the position of adverb clause in the complex sentence. It occupies a separate place or position of its own. For instance: a)When the cat is away, the mice will play. B) Where there is a will, there is a way. c) As you sow, so will you reap. But it does not happen in all cases. For instance: I take medicine so that I can be cured. I am as tall as my younger brother (is). C) You cannot succeed unless you work hard. The old man is so weak that he cannot walk. So it not correct to say that subordinate adverb clause has a separate identity with a comma from the principal clause. As explained above there may not be comma in between the principal clause and subordinate adverb clause. It may not have a separate identity.

One thing is very important that the subordinate clause in the relevant complex sentence functions as an adverb functions in a complex sentence. It is to be noted and kept in mind. It is, therefore, necessary to know about the functions of adverb.

Let us learn the function of adverb and that of the subordinate clause that also functions as adverb and that is why it is called subordinate adverb clause.

The function of an adverb is explained as follows:

1. Time – Usually begins with these subordinating conjunctions - when, whenever, before, after, till, since, for, while, as soon as. S. Adverb clause normally begins with subordinating conjunction – when. For instance: When the cat is away, the mice will play.

2. Place - where, wherever. S. Adverb Clause stats with where. Where there is a will, there is a way.

3. Purpose – So that, in order that, that. I take medicine so that I can be cured and Reason or Cause – Because, inasmuch as, as, since. My father cannot attend the meeting because he is sick

4. Effect or result – So that, such that. My father is so weak that he cannot stand up.

5. Comparison – Than, as … as, so …as. My elder brother is taller than I (am)

6. Contrast – Though, although, even if, even though. He is honest though he is poor.

7. Manner –As though, as if. As you sow, so will you reap.

8. Condition – Unless, if, in case, provided that. I will not go out of my class if it rains.

Let us analyse some complex sentences:

1. The mice will play. – PC
2. When the cat is away – S. Adverb Clause showing time.
3. There is a way.- PC
4. Where there is a will – S. Adverb Clause showing place.
5. I take medicine. – PC
6. So that I can be cured – S. Adverb Clause showing purpose.
7. I will not go out of the class. – PC
8. If it rains – S. Adverb Clause showing condition.
9. Do hope till now everyone must have followed how to analyse the sentences whether it is a simple sentence or a compound sentence or a mixed sentence or a complex sentence. Now you can understand the structure of each one and can write these sentences correctly.
10. I like to mention here that all subordinate clauses begin with subordinating conjunctions. There may be instances where the subordinating conjunction is hidden or inherent.
11. There is no thumb rule that a subordinate clause begins with a particular subordinating conjunction is a subordinate noun clause or a subordinate adjective clause or a subordinate adverb clause. It will be clear to understand with these examples as follows:

Let us take "where" as one of the subordinating conjunction:

a) Where the principal of my college lives is not known to me.
b) The house where I live in is five miles away from my school.
c) Where there is a will, there is a way.

In all from A) to C) we notice that:

1. Where in A), B) and C) play quite different role in A) the subordinate clause beginning with where is a subordinate noun clause whereas in B) and in C) are subordinate adjective clause and subordinate adverb clause respectively. So it is not correct to say that a particular subordinate clause beginning with a particular subordinating conjunction will be a particular subordinate clause viz. Subordinate noun clause or subordinate adjective clause or subordinate adverb clause. To decide it we should know the rules and only the rules can help you to find out/ pick out any subordinate clause and to name it explaining the reason from the complex sentence correctly. It is true that a subordinating conjunction is a yardstick in helping us in picking out appropriately any subordinate clause from any complex sentence for analysing. It is advised to learn the relevant rule in each case.

Do hope all of you have followed what I have explained above about "Analysis of Sentence" with the suitable examples wherever I felt necessary to quote.

*   *   *

E – ENGLISH GRAMMAR (ANALYSIS ONLY)

Description

Whosoever wants to learn English, he/she has to learn English Grammar. Grammar teaches how to read, write and speak English correctly.

Grammar is divided into five important parts:

1. : Orthography
2. : Etymology
3. : Syntax
4. : Punctuation
5. : Prosody

A learner of English Grammar is taught about alphabet 26 letters – Capital and Small letters separately – how to read, how to write and how to speak (pronounce) these letters nicely with ease.

Then with the joining of one letter to another letter or letters they are taught how to form words step by step. Here also they are taught the method or art how to spell well these letters and how to learn nicely to read, write and speak these words with ease.

At the third stage of teaching they are taught how to make sentence with the help of subject, verb, object and moreover with the complements, if any.

For the students of senior classes they have to learn more about important chapters of Grammar so that they can be able to write the answers of long type questions, essays, letters etc. Over and above some grammar portions are also prescribed in the syllabus/prospectus. As these portions are very important ones and tough also, the students have to pay proper attention to the rules and get them by heart.

These chapters are very important in English grammar:

1. : Kinds of sentence
2. : Parts Of Speech
3. : Tense
4. : Narration – Direct and Indirect Speech
5. : Transformation
6. : Analysis (Clauses)
7. : Synthesis
8. : Punctuation

Analysis is a very important chapter of English Grammar. Analysis means to analyse a complex sentence mainly into two parts – 1 – Principal Clause and 2 – Subordinate Clause with its exact kind i.e. whether it is a Noun Clause or an Adjective Clause or an Adverb Clause.

In this chapter the author has made an attempt in a very simple language with very suitable examples as to how students can understand which part of the sentence is a Principal Clause and which part is a Subordinate Noun Clause or Subordinate Adjective Clause or Subordinate Adverb Clause and why? Students after learning the lesson can easily pick out the clauses from the complex sentence comprising of Principal Clause and Subordinate Noun Clause or Subordinate Adjective Clause or Subordinate Adverb Clause but with appropriate reasons under the rules as stated in the booklet of Analysis – A part of English Grammar.

Do hope students and the boys desirous of learning English can be able to learn this important chapter within a few hours and can mastery over the subject by getting by heart all the relevant rules and practising to pick out clauses and naming them correctly with reasons.

Over and above those people who couldn't learn it in their students' life can also get a golden opportunity of learning this important chapter any time while in leisure particularly on tour waiting for bus, train or flight or when they are in leisure in their houses or in their offices.

Durga Prasad
Author

*   *   *

Analysis

Analysis means to analyze a sentence into different parts and name each sentence or parts of the sentence separately.

Examples:

1. Having gone to market, I bought some books.
2. Dashrath, King of Ayodhya, had four sons.
3. I am here and you are there.
4. I shall give you some money, if you come to my house.
5. When the cat is away, the mice will play.

In two sentences 'bought' and "had" are two finite verbs only having their subjects. The sentence which has only one finite verb is called Simple Sentence.

In sentence no. 3 there are two finite verbs "am" and "are" –two sentences are connected with conjunction "and" and these two sentences are Independent. Such sentence is called Compound Sentence.

In sentences 4 and 5 we find two sentences in each one –one is independent and the other is dependent or subordinate. One part of the sentence has complete sense while the other part has incomplete sense. Such sentence is called Complex Sentence.

Under analysis chapter we learn Clauses. First of all we should know what clauses mean. A clause is a part of a sentence having a finite verb and a subject.

One part of the sentence has complete sense while the other has incomplete sense. The sense of the incomplete sentence depends upon that of the complete sentence. Thus the sentence which has complete sense is called Principal Clause while the other which has incomplete sense is called Subordinate Clause – Subordinate means the sense or meaning of which depends upon the other i.e. on Principal Clause.

In sl.no. 4 we can analyze the sentence as follows:

a) I shall give you some money – Principal Clause.
b) If you come to my house – Subordinate Clause.

In sl. No. 5 we can analyze the sentence as follows:

a) The mice will play – Principal Clause.
b) When the cat is away – Subordinate Clause.

Principal clause or main clause or independent clause is the same.

Subordinate clause or dependent clause is the same.

Normally we know and express as Principal Clause and Subordinate Clause only. These names are very popular amongst the teachers and the students.

First of all we should know how to analyze the sentence (normally complex sentence) into Principal clause and Subordinate Clause.

Let us analyze the sentence and then understand the meaning of each one separately.

1. Where there is a will, there is a way.
2. I will not go out, if it rains.
3. As you sow, so will you reap.
4. I do not know when he will come back.
5. The book, I like most, is the Ramayana.
6. What he did was wrong.
7. Why she is sad is not known to me.
8. All that glitters is not gold.
9. He, that is down, needs fear no fall.
10. This is what I wanted to tell you.
11. The news, that she has come. is true.
12. Your success depends upon how regularly you work hard.

Let us pick out Principal clause and Subordinate Clause one by one from the above sentences.

1. (a) There is a way — Principal Clause.
   (b) Where there is a will — Subordinate Clause.

2. (a) I will not go out — Principal Clause.
   (b) If it rains — Subordinate Clause.

3. (a) As you sow — Subordinate Clause.
   (b) So will you reap — Principal Clause.

4. (a) I do not know — Principal Clause.
   (b) When he will come back — Subordinate Clause.

5. (a) The book is the Ramayana — Principal Clause.
   (b) (Which is inherent here) I like most — Subordinate Clause.

6. (a) (It is inherent here) It was wrong — Principal Clause.
   (b) What he did — Subordinate Clause.

7. 7. (a)-It (It is inherent here) is not known to me — Principal Clause.
   (b) Why she is sad — Subordinate Clause.

8. 8. (a) All is not gold — Principal Clause.
   (b) That glitters — Subordinate Clause.

9. 9. (a) He needs fear no fall — Principal Clause.
   (b) That is down — Subordinate Clause.

10. 10. (a) This is (something is inherent which is not known) — Principal Clause.
    (b) Which I wanted to tell you — Subordinate Clause.

11. 11. (a) The news is true — Principal Clause.
    (b) That she has come — Subordinate Clause.

12. 12. (a) Your success depends upon — Principal Clause.
    (b) How regularly you work hard — Subordinate Clause.

How to recognize a clause from a sentence is not difficult, if one has a basic knowledge of grammar.

Clause= A part of a sentence + subject + finite verb (main verb)

From the above examples one can understand and pick out clauses easily.

In the above examples in every sentence there are two clauses- one is Principle Clause and the other is Subordinate Clause. The Principal Clause is independent whereas the Subordinate Clause is dependent one. The Principle Clause starts with some subject- a noun or pronoun whereas the Subordinate Clause starts with some subordinating conjunction as under:

As, as if, though, although, as though, as much as, as far as, after, before, because, since, that, so that, provided, than, until, unless, lest, and starting with interrogative Pronouns like who, whom, which, how, where, when, why, what, etc. There are numerous subordinating conjunctions which one can know one by one while reading this important chapter of grammar.

Kinds of Clause

There are two kinds of clauses:

1. Principal Clause
2. Subordinate Clause

Subordinate Clause is of three kinds:

1. Subordinate Noun Clause
2. Subordinate Adjective Clause
3. Subordinate Adverb Clause

Principal Clause is the main or independent clause with its subject+ finite verb with complete meaning or sense. For examples:

1. <u>I do not know</u> when he will come back.
2. Where there is a will, <u>there is a way</u>.
3. What he said <u>is true.</u>
4. <u>The news</u> that she has come <u>is true.</u>
5. <u>The house</u> I live in <u>is far away from here.</u>

All the underlined clauses are Principal Clauses because all these have their own subjects in form of nouns or pronouns- all these have their own finite verbs and all these clauses are independent and also have complete meaning or sense.

Subordinate Clause: It has already been explained above elaborately.

1. <u>Subordinate Noun Clause</u>

<u>What is the function of a</u> noun in a sentence is the function of a clause in a sentence. The functions are as follows:

1. <u>Subject to a verb</u>
2. Object to a verb
3. Object to a preposition
4. Complement to a verb
5. In apposition to a noun 1. Subject to a verb

How the subordinate clause is the noun clause?

When the subordinate clause is the subject to the finite verb of the principal clause, it is a noun clause. For example:

a) <u>What he said</u> was not true.
b) <u>Where he lives at</u> is not known.
c) <u>When he will come</u> is uncertain.
d) <u>How the magician played the trick</u> is a mystery.
e) <u>Why she is sad today</u> is not known to anybody.

All the underlined clauses are the Noun Clauses because in all the sentences these subordinate clauses are the subject to the finite verbs of the principal Clauses from sl. No. (a) to (e)

2. Object to a verb

When the subordinate clause is the object to the finite verb of the principal clause, it is a subordinate noun clause. For example:

1. I do not know <u>what he said.</u>
2. I do not know <u>where he lives at.</u>
3. I do not know <u>when he will come.</u>
4. I do not know <u>how the magician played the trick.</u>
5. I do not know <u>why she is sad today.</u>

All the underlined subordinate clauses are the subordinate noun Clauses because these are object to the verbs in the sentence from (1) to (5)

In order to make it clear, I have just reversed the subordinate noun clause – subject to the verb to subordinate noun clause object to the verb. In fact I have played a trick to make the subject easier to understand.

3. Object to a preposition

1. Your success depends upon <u>how sincerely you work hard.</u>
2. Rely on <u>what he says.</u>
3. You must pay for <u>what is worth.</u>
4. Don't believe in <u>what he said.</u>

All the underlined subordinate clauses are the subordinate noun clauses because these are object to the preposition – upon in (1), on in (2), for in (3) and in In (4).

4. Complement to a verb

Complement to a verb means the subordinate clause is complement to the finite verb of the principal clause of the sentence. Complement means coordinating which makes the sentence meaningful. For example:

1. This is <u>what I wanted to tell you.</u>
2. It is <u>what you were looking for.</u>
   In the above cited sentences all the underlined subordinate clauses are the subordinate Noun <u>Clauses because these clauses are actually</u> complement to the verb of the principal clause.

5. In apposition to a noun

Normally the subordinate clause in apposition to a noun starts with subordinating conjunction "that" and this conjunction just succeeds (comes after) a noun of the principal clause of the sentence. For example:

1. The news <u>that he has come</u> is true.
2. The judgment <u>that the judge has delivered</u> is just and right.
3. The statement <u>that the minister has given in the meeting</u> is baseless.

All the underlined clauses are the subordinate noun clauses because these are started with subordinating conjunction "that" and precedes (comes after) the nouns - news, judgment, and statement in the above cited sentences.

2 Subordinate Adjective Clause

Let us understand what an adjective is. Adjective is a word which qualifies a noun or pronoun. In adjective clause also the function of adjective is the same.

When it appears that the subordinate clause qualifies some noun or pronoun of the principal clause, such subordinate clause will be Subordinate Adjective Clause. For example:

1. The house <u>where I live in</u> is well ventilated.
2. The book <u>I like most</u> is the Ramayana.
3. The time <u>which is lost</u> is lost forever.
4. The boy <u>whom I met yesterday</u> is a teacher.
5. The reason <u>why he has left the meeting</u> is not known to me.
6. The year <u>when Mahatma Gandhi was born</u> is 1869.
7. The lady <u>who advised us to be present in the</u> meeting is a political leader.
8. He <u>that is down</u> needs fear no fall.
9. All <u>that glitters</u> is not gold.
10. He <u>who helps himself</u> helps his family.

All the underlined subordinate clauses are the subordinate Adjective Clauses because these qualify their nouns or pronouns in the sentences cited above in principal clauses.

4. Subordinate Adverb Clause

The function of adverb in a sentence is similar to that of clause in a sentence. The functions of adverb are as follows;

A) To express Time
B) To express place
C) To express purpose
D) To express reason
E) To express condition
F) To express effect
G) To express comparison
H) To express contrast
I) To express extent or manner

In order to recognize the adverb subordinate clause

These are the important hints:

1. It starts with subordinating conjunction and always in one side of the sentence. The clause functions as an adverb —means it modifies some verb or adjective or adverb – denoting time, place etc. as cited above.
2. It is neither noun clause nor adjective clause.

For example:

1. Time:

   a) <u>When the cat is away</u>, the mice will play.
   b) The doctor always comes <u>whenever he is called for.</u>
   c) I met a lame man <u>while I was walking in the street.</u>
   d) He awoke <u>after the sun had gone up in the sky.</u>
   e) I will not do it <u>before I take the money.</u>
   f) <u>As soon as I reached the station</u>, the train had left.
   g) <u>No sooner did I reach the station</u> than the train had left.
   h) <u>Since he is a minor</u>, he cannot vote.
   i) Wait <u>as long as I come back.</u>
   j) Wait <u>unless I come back.</u>
   k) Wait <u>until I come back.</u>
   l) You may see me <u>whenever you like.</u>

2. Place:

   a) You must stay <u>wherever you are.</u>
   b) He will be arrested <u>wherever he goes.</u>

3. Purpose:

   a) He works hard <u>that he may pass the examination.</u>
   b) My mother took medicine <u>that she might get well.</u>
   c) Walk carefully <u>lest you should stumble.</u>
   d) He reads regularly <u>so that he may get through the examination.</u>

4. Reason:

    a) I can help you <u>because you are poor</u>.
    b) <u>Since you are late</u>, you will not be allowed in the examination hall.
    c) I will not go out <u>as it rains heavily</u>.

5. Condition:

    a) We will not go out, <u>if it rains today.</u>
    b) You will not get through the exam, <u>unless you work hard.</u>
    c) you will not be given a prize, <u>in case you fail to come in time.</u>
    d) <u>Whether you are happy or unhappy,</u> I will not allow you to stay in my room.

There are some adverbial clauses which do not have adverbial conjunctions, even then they are adverb clauses.

1) <u>Had you studied well</u>, you would not have failed.
    In another words the sentence will be:
    <u>If</u> you would study, you would not have failed.

2) *I would be happy <u>were I rich.</u>*
    Or I would be happy <u>if I were rich</u>.

3) Some clauses start with whatever, however, whichever, whatsoever, whenever. For example:

    a) <u>Whatsoever you may be,</u> you cannot abuse me.
    b) <u>However wisely you may act</u>, you will not succeed in your mission.
    c) <u>Whichever road you proceed</u>, you shall not reach in time.
    d) <u>Whenever you come to my house</u>, you are always welcome.

6. <u>Effect:</u>

<u>Normally</u> Adverb Clause starts with "that or so that" to show effect. For example:

a) He is such a gentleman that everybody respects him.
b) He is so good a postman that all love him.
c) So timely he reached the destination that he won the race.
d) So sincerely he worked that he was promoted within a year.

7. Comparision:

In the sentence a comparison is made from one person or thing to another person or thing - one is the principal clause and the other is subordinate adverb clause starting with "than, as. For example:

a) He likes you more than (he likes) me.
b) He likes you more than I (like you)
c) You are wiser than you look.
d) I am not such a fool as you think.

8. Contrast:

a) Though he is poor, he is honest.
b) You will never be happy however rich you may be.
c) I was not honored notwithstanding that I discharged my duty very sincerely.

9. Manner:

Men will reap as they sow.
As men sow so will they reap.

10. Extent:

a) So far as I know, he is a very good man.
Till now you have learnt a lot about analysis and can understand clauses and can be able to write complex sentences correctly and confidently having at least one principal clause and one or more than one subordinate clauses. You will have to learn analysis, if you want to learn English language and literature.

*   *   *

E – ENGLISH GRAMMAR (SYNTHESIS OF SENTENCE ONLY)

Description

Synthesis of Sentence means to combine or join two or more than two sentences into a single (one) sentence without changing the sense of the sentences that are being combined together as per the rules of Grammar.

The author keeping in view the rules of grammar has explained or described so elaborately the various methods of combining or joining sentences in such a simple language with suitable examples that anyone be able to learn it at ease.

Moreover one can enrich his knowledge in a very short time too.

Durga Prasad
Author

*   *   *

Synthesis of Sentences

It is one of the most important chapters of English Grammar which teaches us how to combine one or more than one sentences into a single one keeping in view the very sense or meaning of the same. Although the structure of the different sentences changes into one sentence but the sense remains the same. Sometimes we have to express the same thing but in short and when more than one sentences are combined together, it becomes a single sentence. **The method or process that we adopt in shortening the sum and substance of a number of sentences into a single one, is termed as "Synthesis of Sentence".**

Thus we can define synthesis as a systematic process to combine at least two or more sentences into one sentence. The sentences so combined may be simple or compound or complex ones. Here it is noted that any two or more than two sentences irrespective of its kinds – simple, compound or complex may be combined as per the rules of the grammar.

The very purpose of synthesis is to brief or shorten or precise the matter. It helps us in writing better English and to express our ideas or experiences in a better way while writing a bigger sentence in lieu of so many sentences using so many subjects, objects and compliments time and again.

English is a very rich language spoken almost all over the countries of the world. It is recognised as an international language because of its simplicity as well as variety of uses in various ways so suitably that one cannot imagine even. It is so popular that everyone is desirous of learning its language and literature at all cost.

Obviously there are some rules of synthesis. There are certain methods we have to learn to synthesize different sentences of different forms to a single one in such a way that the sense or meaning remains the same. Sometimes we need to express our views in the shortest way as far as possible and here only the rules of synthesis help us to serve our very purpose. At the same time it is not true the methods or rules that we follow are solely, wholly and exclusively are as those of mathematics. To combine two or more than two sentences into a single one must have a good command over word-power and must be aware of English language and literature to a satisfactory extent. Moreover he/she has the sufficient knowledge of different chapters of grammar i.e. kinds of sentence according to sense and according to form, parts of speech, tense, analysis of sentence, transformation of sentence, narration, syntax, punctuation etc.

The author has tried his level best to teach the learners all these important chapters of grammar through his E-Blue Books duly published in Google Play and are available for reading by paying a small amount online.

Whatever the shortfalls are there, we will explain the rules or methods of synthesis for the learners. There is no exaggeration to say that the learners can be able to combine sentences after reading this chapter thoroughly.

The rules or methods are elucidated as follows:

1. **By using "Participles"**
2. **By using "Infinitives"**
3. **By using "Nominative Absolute"**
4. **By using "Noun or clause or phrase in Apposition"**
5. **By using "Preposition with a noun or gerund"**
6. **By using an "Adverb or Adverbial phrase or Subordinate Adverb Clauses"**

1. **By using Participles:** In fact to join sentences into a single one by using participles is very easy. One has to learn the rules only. **Participles are divided into two parts – one present participle and the other past participle**. The rules concerning to each are slightly different.

   It will be clear to understand with the examples that are given below:

   i) He found Rs.5. He went to market. He bought a pen. Here we notice three simple sentences one after another and all these sentences are in past tense and the subjects in all these sentences are one and the same. Now we can combine these sentences into a single one by following present participle as well as past participle.

   A) **By using present participle:**
      He, finding Rs.5, going to market, bought a pen.
   B) **By using past participle:**
      He, having found Rs.5, having gone to market, bought a pen.
      Akbar ruled India for more than 50 years. He fought so many battles. He defeated many kings. He died in 1605.

   A) By using present participle:

Akbar, ruling India for more than 50 years, fighting so many battles, defeating many kings, died in 1605.

B) By using past participle: Akbar, having ruled India for more than 50 years, having fought so many battles, having defeated many kings, died in 1605.

The rules relating to it are as follows:

A) We can use participles only when the incidents happened one after one or one after another in the past tense.
B) The finite verb of the last sentence should be kept in the last and the incidents that happened before should be changed into either in present participle or in past participle as deems suitable.
C) All the sentences must have the same subject.
   In joining the sentences as given above we have followed the rules in toto.

2. **By using Infinitives:**

It is also an important rule that we follow and combine sentences unhesitatingly. At the same time it is also very easy to understand and easy to combine sentences.

We use infinitives to join sentences when incidents happen at a time and we find co-relation with each other or one another. Moreover there may be the relation of cause or effect or purpose. Sometimes the subjects are different and sometimes not at all but in both the cases we can join the sentences following the rules.

It will be clear to understand when we notice the examples:

A) His house was sold. He had to pay his debts.
   His house was sold to pay his debts.
B) He is too weak. He cannot walk.
   He is too weak to walk.
C) You must finish this exercise. There are still ten sums.
   You have still ten sums of this exercise to finish.
D) Your brother has some bills. He must pay.
   Your brother has some bills to pay.
E) She goes to market. She has to buy a book.
   She goes to market to buy a book.

3. **By using Nominative Absolute:**

We often use Nominative Absolute to join sentences:

A) When different subjects are found in sentences.
B) When incidents happen one after another and there is a relation of action and effect between them.

i) The Sun rose. The fog disappeared.
    The Sun having risen, the fog disappeared.
ii) His wife arrived. He was very pleased.
    His wife having arrived, he was very pleased.
iii) The hunter fired his gun. He missed the aim. The tiger jumped upon him.
    He having fired his gun, having missed the aim, the tiger jumped upon him.
iv) The accused was questioned. No witness came forward. The judge dismissed the case.
    The accused having been questioned, having no witness come forward, the judge dismissed the case.

4. **By using Noun or phrase in apposition:**

By the help of Noun or phrase in apposition we can join sentences easily. It is used when the things so said in a sentence are described or explained about the quality of a person, place or thing in other sentences.

i) Dr. Rajendra Prasad was elected president of India. He was a great scholar. He was a freedom fighter.
    Dr. Rajendra Prasad was elected president of India, a great scholar and freedom fighter.
    Note: Here a great scholar and freedom fighter is the description or explanation of the first sentence about Dr. Rajendra Prasad.
ii) Rabindranath Tagore's most famous book is Gitanjali. It is a collection of short poems.
    Rabindranath Tagore's most famous book Gitanjali, is a collection of short poems.
    Note: A collection of short poems explains or describes Gitanjali.

iii) Coal is a very important mineral. It is hard, black and bright.

Coal, hard, black and bright, is a very important mineral.

Note: Here the second sentence explains or describes coal – a noun only.

iv) The cow gives milk. Milk is a nutritious thing.

The cow gives milk, a nutritious thing.

Note: A nutritious thing says about the quality of a thing.

v) The dog bit the man. He was a notorious burglar.

The dog bit the man, a notorious burglar.

Note: A notorious burglar describes the noun – the man in the first sentence.

5. **By using Preposition with a noun or a gerund:** By using preposition with a Noun or Gerund also helps to combine two or more than two simple sentences into a single one, but there is no exact rule for it. The learners should apply their own knowledge and wit while joining the sentences. Some of the examples can help the learners to understand the process as to how they can combine conveniently two or more sentences into a single one.

i) Her husband died. She heard the news. She fainted.

On hearing the news of her husband's death she fainted.

ii) He has failed many times. Still he hopes to succeed.

In spite of failures many times he hopes to succeed.

iii) He could not attend his class. He was seriously ill.

He could not attend his class, for he was seriously ill.

iv) She remained there for hours together. She did not move anywhere. She did not speak anything.

She remained there for hours together without moving anywhere or speaking anything.

v) My son was selected in army. He worked hard.

My son was selected in army by dint of hard work.

6. **By using Adverb or Adverbial phrases or clauses:** At least two or more than two sentences can be combined together by using an adverb or adverbial phrases or adverb subordinate clause. The examples cited below can help the learners to understand it well:

i) He is not a good boy. It is certain.
Certainly he is not a good boy.
ii) The train is very late. That is usual.
Usually the train is very late.
iii) I got the first prize. I was fortunate.
Fortunately I got the first prize.
iv) The Sun already set. The labourers did not finish their job.
The labourers did not finish their job even by Sunset.
v) He kicked the goalkeeper. It was his intention to do so.
Intentionally he kicked the goalkeeper.
vi) I reached the station. The train had left.
As soon as I reached the station, the train had left.
Or No sooner did I reach the station the train had left.
Or the train had left before I reached the station.
vii) The cat is away. The mice will play.
When the cat is away, the mice will play.

Over and above there are some other methods for combining very easily two or more than two sentences.

1. **By using co-ordinating conjunctions**
2. **By using subordinating conjunctions**

By using co-ordinating conjunction: First of all let us understand conjunction. A conjunction is a word which is used to join or combine words, phrases or sentences. Here we will talk about joining two or more than two sentences. If so then we should know about co-ordinating conjunction.

A conjunction which is used to join two or more than two sentences is called a co-ordinating conjunction.

Again such conjunctions are divided into different types depending upon their characteristics or features:

A) Cumulative Conjunctions:

i) And: It is commonly used to join sentences.
Come here. I will give you a toffee.
Come here and I will give you a toffee.

ii) As well as: Tagore wrote poems. He wrote short stories.
Tagore wrote poems as well as short stories.

iii) Not only ... but also: He is not only a cricketer, but an actor also.

B) Adversative conjunctions: Which one is opposite to one statement to other. But, still, yet, while, whereas are such conjunctions.

i) She is beautiful. She is shrewd. She is beautiful but shrewd.
ii) He got the second prize. He is not happy. He got the second prize still he is not happy.
iii) He was upgraded. He was not satisfied. He was upgraded yet he was not satisfied.
iv) He is punctual. His brother is always late. He is punctual whereas his brother is always late.
v) You love me. Your sister hate me. You love me while your sister hate me.

C) Alternative conjunctions: where there is a choice to choose between the two alternatives: They are or, either ... or. neither ... nor, otherwise, else, lest.

i) You can argue the case yourself. You can authorise me to argue your case. You can argue yourself or you can authorise me to argue your case.
ii) Show me your identity proof. If not pay me the fine. Show me either your identity proof or pay me the fine.
iii) She doesn't appear to be my wife. She doesn't appear to be her sister. She appears neither to be my wife nor her sister.
iv) You must obey the traffic rules. If not you will be fined. You must obey the traffic rules otherwise you will be fined.
v) You will have to pay the premium in time. If not you will have to pay interest. You will have to pay the premium in time, else you will have to pay interest.
vi) Walk carefully. You should not stumble. Walk carefully lest you should stumble.

D) Illative conjunctions: Which express an inference: For (when used in lieu of because), so, therefore are used as illative conjunctions:

   i)   My son couldn't attend his class yesterday. He was suffering from headache. My son couldn't attend his class yesterday, for he was suffering from headache.

   ii) It was raining. He couldn't go out of his house. It was raining, so he couldn't go out of his house.

   iii) I am going to Patna tomorrow. I may please be granted casual leave for two days. I am going to Patna tomorrow, therefore I may please be granted casual leave for two days.

     Note: In all such cases/matters normally two sentences are joined together.

2. By using subordinating conjunctions: A conjunction normally used to join two different statements out of which one is subordinate or dependent (Here the complete sense or meaning of the subordinate clause) on the other (Here the principal or main clause) is called a subordinating conjunction. Such subordinate clause begins with a subordinating conjunction which helps to join two or more than two sentences. For examples:

   i)   The train is arriving. I do not know the time of arrival. I do not know when the train is arriving.

   ii) He lives somewhere. I do not know it. I do not know where he lives.

   iii) I read a book every morning. It is the Ramayan. The book which I read every morning is the Ramayan.

   iv) What is his name? I do not know. I do not know what his name is.

   v) He had left his hostel. I could know the reason. I could not know the reason why he had left his hostel.

   vi) I like Mrinal most. He is a good student. The student whom I like most is Mrinal.

Do hope you have learnt the methods of joining two or more than two sentences and be benefitted with it.

*   *   *

E – ENGLISH GRAMMAR (TRANSFORMATION OF SENTENCE ONLY)

Description

Transformation of Sentence: It is a very important chapter of English Grammar as we find option for expressing our views in more than one way. That is why everyone should learn the necessary methods/rules as to how one sentence can be transformed or changed into another sentence without changing the sense or meaning of the earlier one.

It widens the scope of using it as suitably as possible.

This chapter describes as follows:

1. **From Affirmative to Interrogative Sentence**
2. **From Negative to Interrogative Sentence**
3. **From Affirmative to Negative Sentence**
4. **From Exclamatory to Assertive Sentence**
5. **Remove – "Too"**

The subject is explained with suitable examples so that the learners can understand it thoroughly.

Durga Prasad
Author

*   *   *

Transformation of Sentence

A) From Affirmative to Interrogative
B) From Negative to Interrogative
C) From Affirmative to Negative
D) From Exclamatory to Assertive
E) Remove "Too"

Transformation of Sentence means to change one sentence into another without changing the sense or meaning.

From Assertive to Interrogative Sentence or vice - versa:
Since Assertive Sentence is divided into Affirmative and Negative sentences, we will explain how to change from affirmative to interrogative and negative to interrogative ones one by one. Some of the examples are given below to understand as to how one sentence is changed into another without changing the sense or meaning.

A) From Affirmative to Interrogative Sentence:

i) All human beings are mortal. To Interrogative
Are all human beings not mortal? Aren't all human beings mortal?

ii) Everyone loves his country. To Interrogative
Who does not love his country?

iii) Everyone would run from a lion. To interrogative
Who would not run from a lion?

iv) They were warned for being naughty. To Interrogative
Were they not warned for being naughty?

v) Man is mortal. To Interrogative
Is man not mortal?

vi) He is blind of an eye. To Interrogative
   Is he not blind of an eye? – Isn't he blind of an eye?

vii) You can jump into the river. To Interrogative
   Can't you jump into the river?

Note: The negative word like – not or no + sign of interrogation at the end of sentence i.e. interrogative sentence makes the sentence positive or affirmative.

B) From Negative to Interrogative Sentence:

i) No one can put up with such conduct. – To Interrogative
   Can anyone put up with such conduct?

ii) A man cannot live forever. To Interrogative
   Can a man live forever?

iii) I shall never forget those happy days. – Interrogative
   Shall I ever forget those happy days?

iv) No one can bear such an insult. To Interrogative
   Can anyone bear such an insult?

v) The leopard cannot change its sports. – To Interrogative
   Can the leopard change its sports?

vi) I can never forget him. To Interrogative
   Can I ever forget him?

C) From Affirmative to Negative Sentences:

i) Only a burglar can do that. – None but a burglar can do that.
ii) Man is mortal. – Man is not immortal.
iii) She is more beautiful than her elder sister. – Her elder sister is not as beautiful as she.

iv) Iron is heavier than cotton. – Cotton is not as heavy as iron.

v) I have a little knowledge about inflation. – I do not have much knowledge about inflation.

vi) I am doubtful of his success. – I am not sure of his success.

vii) She is always punctual. – She is never late.

viii) As soon as I called him, he fled away. – No sooner did I call him than he fled away.

ix) Only the evening star has appeared. – None but the evening star has appeared.

x) Only a fool would talk like this. – None but a fool would talk like this.

xi) We tried every plan. – We left no plan untried.

xii) We will always remember them. – We will never forget them.

Note: It is a general rule that one negative word nullifies the other positive word and thus the sense becomes positive or affirmative one. For instance in the given examples we find "always" against "never" and "punctual" against "late."

D) From Exclamatory to Assertive Sentences:

Exclamatory Sentence is that in which one expresses his emotional feeling about a person or a place or a thing all of a sudden. It comes out of the mouth all of a sudden what he/she feels in his/her mind. The expression may be related to pleasure or sorrow or wonder or contempt or imagination or shyness etc.

Exclamatory sentence normally starts with an exclamatory word like – how, what, O that, hurrah, alas, if, would that, oh, fie, fie etc. and ends in with an exclamatory sign instead of a full stop. The exclamatory sentence very often remains incomplete but one can understand the sense or meaning of the sentence and on the basis of that he/she transforms such sentences easily into assertive sentence. For instance:

i) How beautiful the scene is!

ii) What a foolish boy!

iii) O that it may rain whole day!

iv) Hurrah! We have won the match.

v) Alas! We have lost the game.

vi) If I were a king of this state!

vii) Would that I could be a woman like you!

viii) Oh! I were a child once again!

We can transform all these exclamatory sentences into assertive sentences as follows:

i)   The scene is very beautiful.

ii) He is a very foolish boy.

iii) I wish that it may rain whole day.

iv) It is a matter of pleasure that we have won the match.

v)   It is a matter of sorrow that we have lost the game.

vi) I wish I could be a king of this state.

vii) I wish that I could be a woman like you.

viii) I wish that I was a child once again.

In all these sentences we do not notice any sign of exclamation at the end of these sentences. Each sentence bears complete sense or complete meaning and there is a full stop at the end of each sentence. The sense or meaning of the exclamatory sentences after changing into assertive ones also remain the same. Similarly we can change the assertive sentences into exclamatory ones following the rules of grammar.

E) Remove – "Too"

Remove – "Too" is also an important part of Transformation of Sentence. A few sentences are such in which "too" is used followed by infinitive 'to' and such sentences are simple sentences. When we have to remove 'too', we should follow the rules as given below:

1.   While removing 'too' 'so' is used in its place i.e. 'too' is substituted by 'so' and in place of infinitive 'to' 'that' is used. Thus the simple sentence is changed into a complex sentence. The tense of the simple sentence remains the same i.e. if the simple sentence is in present tense, the tense of the complex sentence remains the same but if in the past tense, then the tense also changes into past tense. For instance:

i)   The old man is too weak to walk.

ii) The weather is too cold to go out.

iii) The sum is too difficult to solve.

iv) The field is too wetted to play football.

v) The boy is too lazy to work.

vi) The woman is too unable to stand up.

vii) The task is too difficult for us to complete in a day.

viii) The syllabus is too vast for me to finish in a year.

We observe as follows:

All are the simple sentences with a single finite verb – 'is'. The sentences are in present tense. As such there will be no change in the sentence after removal of 'too'. Now 'too' is removed from the above sentences:

i) The old man is so weak that he cannot walk.

ii) The weather is so cold that one cannot go out.

iii) The sum is so difficult that one cannot solve.

iv) The field is so wetted that one cannot play football.

v) The boy is so lazy that he cannot work.

vi) The woman is so unable that she cannot stand up.

vii) The task is so difficult that we cannot complete.

viii) The syllabus is so vast that I cannot complete in a year.

We notice as follows:

i) 'too' is substituted by 'so'.

ii) 'that' is used as subordinating conjunction after the principal clause.

iii) The suitable pronouns have been used in the subordinate clauses.

iv) Since all the sentences are in present tense, the tense of all the sentences remains the same.

v) Infinitive 'to' has disappeared as it is improper to use it after 'cannot'.

vi) In serial nos. ii), iii) and iv) the exact subjects are unknown and as such 'one' is used in each sentence as its subject.

vii) In serial no. vii) we find "for us" as a hint after the adjective, as such in the subordinate clause "we" is used as a subject. Similarly in serial no. viii) we find "for me", as such in the subordinate clause "I" is used as a subject.

viii) The pronoun of the subordinate clause must agree to that of the principal clause in number, gender and person. We find in serial nos.

v) and vi) that 'he' and 'she' are used respectively for 'the boy' and for 'the woman'.

ix) In case the simple sentence is in past tense, the tense of the subordinate clause will also change into past tense. Here in place of 'cannot' 'could not' only is used.

For instance:

i) The old man was too weak to walk.
    After removal of 'too':
    The old man was so weak that he could not walk.
    Similarly the same rule will apply in similar cases also.

If we do not notice any infinitive 'to' after the adjective so used in the simple sentence, we change 'too' into 'very' straightway. For instance:

i)   The hunter is too cruel.
ii) He is too selfish.
iii) The weather is too cold.
iv) The lady was too timid.
v)   he dog was too faithful.

We can remove 'too' in such cases by changing 'too' into 'very' straightway.

i)   The hunter is very cruel.
ii) He is very selfish.
iii) The weather is very cold.
iv) The lady was very timid.
v)   The dog was very faithful.

Note: In the former case 'too' is in the negative sense whereas in the present case it is in positive sense.

It is suggested to understand the sense of the sentence containing 'too' and then one can remove 'too' with ease.

*   *   *

E – ENGLISH GRAMMER (VOICE CHANGE ONLY)

Description

Voice Change is an important part of "Transformation of Sentence" in which one sentence is changed into another but the sense or meaning of one sentence when changed to another remains the same.

It is a rare significance of any language and literature that the speaker can express his/her views not only in one way but in more than one ways also. There is no exaggeration to say it is an art of such a language that enriches it. Voice change is one of them that teaches us how to express our views suitably in both voices - active and passive as and when required on different occasions.

The language in which it is written is very simple, the method that is adopted with the suitable examples is very clear and the flow that once starts with in the beginning continues till it ends in like a fairy tale.

Durga Prasad
Author

*   *   *

Voice Change

In English Grammar voice is of two kinds – (1) – Active Voice and (2) Passive Voice.

Voice Change from active to passive is an important part of "Transformation of Sentence." If change is made from one voice to another, the meaning or sense of the sentence remains the same.

The rules of voice change are as follows:

1. The verb in the active or passive voice should be transitive verb i.e. the effect of action should be on its object, not on its subject. For instance eat, drink, read, write, beat, kill are the transitive verbs as the effect of action is exclusively on its object inasmuch as all these verbs have their own objects whereas weep, laugh, rise, sleep, run, jump, fall, sit, stand, walk are the intransitive verbs. In all such cases the effect of action is on subjects, not on objects and as such voice change either from active to passive or vice versa in later cases cannot be made as per the rules of the grammar.

2. Keeping in view the rules as stated above now we can learn the necessary rules as to how we can change the sentence from active to passive voice and from passive to active voice:

3. When we change from active to passive voice, we have to change the form of the verb from present or past or future tense of the verb into that of the past participle of the verb. For instance (a) I write a letter or (b) I wrote a letter or (c) I shall write a letter – in all these sentences "write" is the transitive verb and while changing from active to passive voice in all cases "write" will be changed into "written" which is the past participle form of the transitive verb "write" and thus the sentences as stated above from (a) to (c) in passive voice will be:

   a) A letter is written by me.
   b) A letter was written by me.
   c) A letter will be written by me.

Now from the above examples it is clear that while transforming from active to passive voice the transitive verb used in active voice is subject to change into past participle form.

4. Here it is worth noting that in passive voice the structure of the sentence is changed but the meaning or sense remains the same.

5. The most important aspects of the rule while changing from active to passive are the changes in place of its subject as well as that of its object in form of noun or pronoun. So far as the noun as subject is concerned, it remains the same either in active voice or in passive voice, I mean to say that there is no change at all in noun as subject or object.

6. One thing is also important that the article – a or an or the or any adjective that precedes its noun or pronoun will precede while changing from active to passive voice or vice versa.

7. While changing from active to passive or vice versa the general rule is that that the subject takes the place of object and the object the place of subject.

For instance:

John writes a letter. Here the subject is John and the object is a letter. If I change it into passive voice, the sentence will be: A letter is written by John. Now we notice that the subject takes the place of the object and the object that of its subject.

8. When we find a pronoun as subject of the sentence in active voice or a pronoun as object in active or passive voice, the pronouns so used either in active or passive voices are changed as per the rule shown in the list as follows:

List of pronouns that change while changing from active voice to passive voice or vice versa:

A) I to me or me to I
B) We to us or us to we
C) You to you or you to you
D) He to him or him to he
E) She to her or her to she
F) They to them or them to they.
G) It, this, that, these, those, remain the same in both the voices i.e. as a subject or as an object.

9. While changing into passive "by" is used before the object.
There is an interchange of places of subject and object in voice change from one to another. For instance:

1. I eat a mango. In passive voice the sentence will be – A mango is eaten by me. Here we find that the subject takes the place of the object and similarly the object takes the place of the subject.
Now it is easy to learn voice change if we go by tense in Assertive Sentences (Affirmative and Negative Sentences):

1. Present Tense:

   a) Present Indefinite Tense:
   I eat a mango. – A mango is eaten by me. (Passive Voice)
   b) Present Imperfect or continuous Tense:
   I am eating a mango. – A mango is being eaten by me. (Passive Voice)
   c) Present Perfect Tense: I have eaten a mango. – A mango has been eaten by me. (Passive Voice)

2. Past Tense:

   a) Past Indefinite: I ate a mango. – A mango was eaten by me. (Passive Voice)
   b) Past Imperfect or continuous: I was eating a mango. – A mango was being eaten by me. (Passive Voice)
   c) Past Perfect: I had eaten a mango. – A mango had been eaten by me. (Passive Voice)

3. Future Tense:

   a) Future Indefinite: I shall eat a mango. – A mango will be eaten by me. (Passive Voice)
   b) Future Imperfect or continuous: Future Imperfect or Continuous tense cannot be changed into passive voice.
   c) Future Perfect: I shall have eaten a mango. – A mango will have been eaten by me. (Passive Voice)

Note: There is no change from active to passive voice if the sentences are either in present, past or future perfect continuous tenses.

In some of the cases "To be" verb is used while changing from active voice to passive voice particularly in cases of Model Auxiliaries verbs. For instance:

A) I can teach you. – You can be taught by me. (Passive Voice)
B) I could teach you. – You could be taught by me. (Passive Voice)
C) I may beat you. – You may be beaten by me. (Passive Voice)
D) I might kill you. – You might be killed by me. (Passive Voice)
E) We should punish the accused. – The accused should be punished by us. (Passive Voice) or we ought to keep our houses clean. – Our houses ought to be kept clean by us. (Passive Voice)
F) We must expel the students who use unfair means. – The students who use unfair means must be expelled by us. (Passive Voice)
G) We are to or have to punish him. – He is to or has to be punished by us. (Passive Voice)

Sometimes we are confused when we find two objects after the transitive verb – one is a direct object and another is an indirect object. In such cases while changing from active voice to passive we can chose any of the object as subject but it must be kept in mind to prefer indirect object to direct object in order to avoid error in changing from active to passive voice. For instance:

1. I teach him English. Here we find two objects – him and English. We should chose him as object. It does not mean that using direct object as subject will be wrong.
Let us see the passive voice in both the cases:

a) Case No. 1. He is taught English by me.
b) Case No. 2. English is taught to him by me.

I understand everyone has followed the difference between the two.
When the sentence in active voice is an interrogative one, the change from active to passive voice will be as follows keeping in view the basic rules of interrogative sentence:

1. Who loves you? – By whom are you loved? (Passive Voice)
2. Who is teaching your sister? – By whom is your sister being taught? (Passive Voice)
3. Who has quoted it? – By whom has it been quoted?

   Likewise we can change from active to passive voice in the remaining tenses following the rules as stated above.

Voice change from active to passive when the sentences are "Imperative Sentences" i.e. in which somebody commands or orders, advises or suggests, requests or forbids someone.

Let us learn it one by one with examples:

1. Command or order:

   Open the door. – Let the door be opened. or you are ordered to open the door. (Passive Voice)
   Close the window. – Let the window be closed. or you are ordered to close the window. (Passive Voice)
   In all such cases where somebody commands or orders someone, the sentence in passive voice starts with "Let" and be as auxiliary verb is used succeeded by past participle form of transitive verb as explained in the examples cited above.

2. Advice or suggestion:

   Take the mobile phone when you go out. – Let the mobile phone be taken when you go out. Or you are advised to take the mobile phone when you go out.(Passive Voice)
   Do not lend money to anyone. – You are advised or suggested not to lend money to anyone. Or you are forbade to lend money to anyone. (Passive Voice)

3. Request:

   Please allow me to leave the meeting. – I may please be allowed to leave the meeting. Or You are requested to allow me to leave the meeting.

Kindly sanction me house building loan. – I may kindly be sanctioned house building loan. Or You are requested to sanction me house building loan.

Or House building loan may kindly be sanctioned to me.

Please sit down. – You are requested to sit down.

Please do not postpone the meeting. – You are requested not to postpone the meeting.

4. Forbid or prohibition:

Do not use unfair means in the examination hall. – You are forbade to use unfair means in the examination hall. Or Unfair means should not be used in the examination hall.

The sentence in passive voice appears to be very useful when we do not want or we are not in a position to disclose the doer. For instance:

a) It is said that honesty is the best policy.
b) It is proved that the earth goes round the Sun.
c) It is presumed that the monsoon will break soon.
d) It is not known where the principal lives at.
e) It is believed that strike will be called off soon.
f) It will be delivered the moment the necessary order is placed.
g) It is certified that Mr. A.K. Gupta was suffering from fever.
h) It is notified that the college will remain closed on good Friday.

The sentence that begins with "Let", the auxiliary verb "Be" is used in passive, other rules remaining the same.

a) Let the president hoist the national flag. – Let the national flag be hoisted by the president.
b) Let him inaugurate the opening ceremony of the call centre. – Let the opening ceremony of the call centre be inaugurated by him.
c) Let us constitute a relief committee to help the needy people of the society. – Let a relief committee be constituted to help the needy people of the society by us.

d) Let us lodge a complaint against the shopkeeper. – Let a complaint be lodged against the shopkeeper by us.

Do hope all of you have followed me and have learnt to change the sentences from active voice to passive voice and moreover have learnt its usage in English language and literature.

*   *   *

E – ENGLISH GRAMMAR (DEGREE CHANGE ONLY)

Description

Degree Change is an important part of "Transformation of Sentence" in which one sentence is changed into another but the sense or meaning of one sentence when changed to another sentence remains the same.

It is a rare significance of any language and literature that the speaker can express his/her views not only in one way/style/fashion but in more than one ways/styles/fashions also. **There is no exaggeration to say that it is an art of such a language that enriches it.** Degree change is one of them that teaches us how to express our views suitably in different degrees – positive, comparative and superlative as and where required on different occasions.

Anyone who desires to learn it can access to "Google Play" and search the related site by typing "Durga Prasad" or "Shubham Kumar" in search column.

"Description" and "About the Author" are free of cost to access but to read the total subject one has to pay Rs.30 online.

The language in which it is written is very simple, the method that is adopted with the suitable examples is very clear and the flow that once starts with in the beginning continues till it ends in like a fairy tale.

The author is the founder of "E-Blue Books." The idea of writing such a book in a few pages was generated when the author was waiting for more than four hours for the second flight from Delhi to Varanasi after arriving from Pune. And thus about 80 such books are published till now in "Google Play" on different topics of different categories in Hindi as well as in English languages for those who have to wait for hours together in airport, rly. Platforms, bus stands and so on. They can pass their time usefully by reading such E-Blue Books in case they have got in -hand facilities to internet connectivity.

Durga Prasad
Author

*   *   *

Degree change

First of all let us understand degree. Degree is a state or position of an adjective in a sentence. For instance:

1. No other student is as wise as Mathew (is).
2. No other girl is as beautiful as Rosy (is).
3. Cotton is not as heavy as iron (is).
4. Mathew is not as tall as John (is).
5. Silver is not as costly as gold (is).

In all the sentences from 1 to 5 the adjectives which are used are wise, beautiful, heavy, tall and costly and these are in their original forms of adjectives. Such an adjective is in its positive degree or state. When we change the sentence in the comparative degree to compare one person to another or one place to another or one thing to another, we change the sentence of the positive degree to the comparative degree and to do so we have to change the adjective in its original form to that of comparative degree and for that we have to follow some rules of grammar.

In case the adjective in its original form i.e. in the positive degree we have to add – er, if the adjective word is in a single (one) syllable and if more than one syllable, more precedes such an adjective. If the adjective word ends in e as in wise, large, only r is added to make the adjective in the form of comparative degree. For instance from wise to wiser, from large to larger, from big to bigger (As per rule g is doubled), from small to smaller, from tall to taller, from short to shorter, from high to higher, from poor to poorer, from rich to richer, from heavy to heavier, from ugly to uglier (Here y is changed into i and er is added as per the rule of the grammar.) and so on …

Again as stated above from popular to more popular, from beautiful to more beautiful, from intelligent to more intelligent, from laborious to more laborious and so on …

Degree change is a part of "Transformation of Sentence" as we find in "Voice Change". In all changes from one to another, the structure or pattern of the sentence changes but the sense or meaning remains the same. It is one of the qualities of the language that we are able to express our views or thought in other way or ways too.

We can change or convert the positive degree to comparative degree or superlative degree with changing the structure of sentence in order to keeping the sense or meaning intact i.e. without changing the sense or meaning.

Let us change the sentences from 1 to 5 in the positive degree cited above to the comparative degree:

1. Mathew is wiser than any other student.
2. Rosy is more beautiful than any other girl.
3. Iron is heavier than cotton.
4. John is taller than Mathew.
5. Gold is costlier than silver.

Then comes the superlative degree. Here also we change the form of the adjective by adding est or most in case the adjective is in more than a single or one syllable. For instance:

Wise to wisest, large to largest, weak to weakest when the adjective is in a single or one syllable and when more than a single syllable, most is used before such an adjective in its original form.

It may be noted that article "the" precedes the adjective in its superlative degree of adjective in all such cases.

Let us change the sentences from 1 to 5 to superlative degree:

1. Mathew is the wisest student.
2. Rosy is the most beautiful girl.
3. In such cases degree change is possible only from positive to comparative or vice versa.
4. Same as above.
5. Same as above.

Let us examine the following sentences which are quite different from the above examples from 1 to 5:

1. Mathew is one of the wisest students of all.
2. Kolkata is one of the busiest cities in India.
3. Rosy is one of the most beautiful girls of all.

One important thing may be noted that "when one of the busiest or like word of any adjective is used in the superlative degree, the noun that follows it, is always in plural number". It is obvious from serial nos.1 to 3 as explained just above - "students, cities and girls are in their plural number.

Let us change these sentences into comparative degree and positive degree.

1. Very few students are as wise as Mathew (is). (Changed from the superlative degree to positive degree) To write "is" at the end of the sentence is not necessary.
2. Mathew is wiser than most other students. (Changed from superlative degree to comparative degree)

1. Very few cities in India are as busy as Kolkata (is). (Changed from superlative degree to positive degree) To write "is" at the end of the sentence is mendatory
2. Kolkata is busier than most other cities in India. (Changed from superlative degree to comparative degree)

1. Very few girls are as beautiful as Rosy (is). (Changed from superlative degree to positive degree) To write "is" at the end of the sentence is not necessary.
2. Rosy is more beautiful than most other girls. (Changed from superlative degree to comparative degree)

It may be noted when we compare from one person to another, one place to another and one thing to another, there will be interchange of degree only from positive to comparative degree or vice versa. There will be no interchange to superlative degree. For instance:

1. Mohan is taller than Sohan. (Comparative degree)
2. Sohan is not as tall as Mohan is. (Positive degree)

1. Kolkata is busier than Patna. (Comparative degree)
2. Patna is not as busy as Kolkata is. (Positive degree)

1. Iron is heavier than cotton. (Comparative degree)
2. Cotton is not as heavy as iron is.

(To write "is" at the end of the sentence in the positive degree is not necessary. Normally it is not written while interchanging to positive degree.

Note: We can use so also in place of as before the adjectives in serial nos. 2 in positive degrees. For instance:

1. Sohan is not so tall as Mohan.
2. Patna is not so busy as Kolkata.
3. Cotton is not so heavy as iron.

It may be noted that "as" or "so" anyone can be used before the adjectives in all positive degrees.

There are some adjectives in original form which are exception to the rule that explained above. They are as follows:

Positive degree	Comparative degree	Superlative degree
Good	better	best
Bad	worse	worst

1. Honesty is the best policy. (Superlative degree)
2. Honesty is better than any other policy. (Comparative degree)
3. No other policy is as good as honesty is. (Positive degree)

1. Ravana was the worst king. (Superlative degree)
2. Ravana was worse than any other king. (Comparative degree)
3. No other kind was as bad as Ravana was. (Positive degree)

In context to the rule explained above the degree interchange from positive to comparative and vice versa only are done in the following cases: For instance:

1. Iron is heavier than cotton.
2. John is taller than Mathew.
3. Gold is costlier than silver.

We can change them into positive degree only, not in the superlative degree.

1. Cotton is not as heavy as iron.
2. Mathew is not as tall as John.
3. Silver is not as costly as gold.

Some useful examples which can be changed from positive to comparative degree only and vice versa.

1. Air is more necessary than food for us to survive. (Comparative degree)
2. Food is not as necessary as air for us to survive. (Positive degree)

1. Krishna is a better dancer than a singer. (Comparative degree)
2. Krishna is not as good a singer as a dancer. (Positive degree)

1. No sooner did I reach the station than the train left. (Comparative degree)
2. As soon as I reached the station, the train left. (Positive degree)

1. It is better to drop than to appear. (Comparative degree)
2. It is not as good to appear as to drop. (Positive degree)

1. It is not more important to get than to give. (Comparative degree)
2. To get is not so important as to give. Or it is not so important to get as to give. (Positive degree)

Do hope till now you have learnt a lot about degree change and now can be able to express your views or thought in the ways or style you like as and where required.

*   *   *

E – ENGLISH GRAMMAR (NARRATION ONLY)

Description

Whosoever wants to learn English, he/she has to learn English Grammar. Grammar teaches how to read, write and speak English correctly.

Grammar is divided into five important parts:

6. : Orthography
7. : Etymology
8. : Syntax
9. : Punctuation
10. : Prosody

A learner of English Grammar is taught about alphabet 26 letters – Capital and Small letters separately – how to read, how to write and how to speak (pronounce) these letters nicely with ease.

Then with the joining of one letter to another letter or letters they are taught how to form words step by step. Here also they are taught the method or art how to spell well these letters and how to learn nicely to read, write and speak these words with ease.

At the third stage of teaching they are taught how to make sentence with the help of subject, verb, object and moreover with the complements, if any.

For the students of senior classes they have to learn more about important chapters of Grammar so that they can be able to write the answers of long type questions, essays, letters etc. Over and above some grammar portions are also prescribed in the syllabus/prospectus. As these portions are very important ones and tough also, the students have to pay proper attention to the rules and learn them properly.

These chapters are very important in English grammar:

9.   : Kinds of sentence
10. : Parts Of Speech
11. : Tense
12. : Narration – Direct and Indirect Speech
13. : Transformation
14. : Analysis (Clauses)
15. : Synthesis
16. : Punctuation

As an English teacher I have experienced that some of the students do not follow when they are taught Narration Chapter i.e. Direct and Indirect Speech and the rules or methods how to change correctly from direct speech or narration to indirect speech or narration.

I am a retired person of nearly 70 years. My sons basically all software engineers working at distant places advised me to write good books for the students out of my long experience of teaching English and my grandson – a student of BCA of Asansol Engineering College, West Bengal (India) has consented to edit the e – books (Booklets) part by part with the least price and get them published.

The Booklet Narration has been written in a very simple language citing suitable examples one by one so that the students can be able to understand or grasp quickly with ease.

Do hope with the publication of this type of book/booklet not only the students but many people who are desirous of learning English can be benefitted particularly they will have enough time/leisure while waiting for bus/train/flight and so on outside with a Smart Phone in their hands with internet connectivity.

Durga Prasad
Author

*   *   *

Narration

Narration means to reproduce or restate something what someone has already stated or said exactly in his or her words or in another words without changing the sense or meaning of his or her statement. Thus we can narrate the statement in two ways-

We can reproduce the statement of someone in the exact words or can reproduce the sense of the statement only. The first method is called Direct Speech or Direct Narration and the second one is called Indirect Speech or Indirect Narration. According to the situation we can adopt any method in expression of what is said by the person.

Narration is a part of Grammar in which the sense or meaning of the sentence does not change while changing direct to indirect narration. Narration is a very important chapter of English Grammar and for good English we must learn it thoroughly.

There are some terminology the meaning of which we must know and learn. Apart from this there are some Rules also which we must get by heart and practice regularly till we do not command over it.

TERMINOLOGY
REPORTIG VERB
REPORTED SPEECH
INVERTED COMMAS
COMMAS
SIGN OF INTERROGATION
PERSON (We change the Pronouns of the Reported Speech as per the necessity)
LIST OF WORDS WHICH CHANGES:
WHILE CHANGING THE SENTENSE
FROM DIRECT SPEECH TO INDIRECT ONE.

For example - (1) Sita said to her father, "I can help you today."
Sita said to her mother," I shall bring your bag today."
"Please sit down here." Said the teacher to the students.
"Do not walk in the sun" said the mum to her child.
"What is your name?" - asked my teacher to me.

The verb used to report something is a reporting verb. The verb –said is a reporting verb.

The sentences within inverted commas are reported speech.

"------------" inverted commas.

Eyes, nose and ears are sense organs. The sign used after eyes is a comma.

What is your name? the sign used after the interrogative sentence is a sign of interrogation.

Person – there are three persons- first person in singular and plural number, second person in singular and plural number and third person in singular and plural number i.e. I, we, thou or you, you, he, she, it, this, they and more than two persons, things etc. these persons change into indirect speech to suit in the sentences of the Indirect speech without changing the sense or the meaning of the sentence in direct speech.

It is very necessary to understand the pronoun for which subject it has been used in the Reporting Verb and accordingly change in the pronoun of the Reported Speech takes place. The same thing applies in case of the object of the Reported Verb the pronoun changes accordingly here also.

What happens while changing the sentence from direct to indirect speech:

The inverted commas in the beginning and at the end of the Direct speech disappear.

The interrogative sign and the exclamatory sign of the Direct speech also disappear and at the end of the sentence only full stop appears.

If the reporting verb is either in Present tense or in Future tense, the tense of the Reported Speech does not change.

If the Reporting Verb is in the Past Tense, the tense of the Reported Speech changes as per the List as follows:

a) Present Indefinite changes to Past Indefinite
b) Present Continuous "   to Past Continuous
c) Present Perfect   "   to Past perfect
d) Present Perfect Continuous to Past PC
e) Past Indefinite to Past perfect
f) Past Continuous to Past PC

Note: Exception: Where the rule does not apply: (a) If in the Reprted Speech the sense of the statement is a Universal Truth, the tense of the

Reported Speech does not change even if the Reporting Verb is in Past Tense. For example-

"Two and two is four."

"Man is mortal"

"The earth is round"

"The sun rises in the east"

"The earth moves round the Sun" (All these reported speech will remain the same.)

List of words which are changed if the Reporting verb is in Past Tense:

Now	to	then
Here	to	there
This	to	that
These	to	those
Today	to	that day
Tonight	to	that night
Tomorrow	to	next day
Yesterday	to	previous day
Next day	to	following day
Come	to	go
Shall	to	should
Will	to	would
Can	to	could
May	to	might
Have	to	had
Has	to	had

Whatever the rules have been explained above, they are the general rules but whatever the rules explained hereunder are the special rules.

In order to change from direct to indirect and to facilitate understanding the methods, the sentences have been divided into 14 parts which will be elucidated one by one.

Rule 1: When the reporting verb is in present or future tenses, the reported speech as an assertive sentence, the tenses of the reported speech will not change.

He says to me, "You are a good boy."

He says to me that I am a good boy.

You will say to me," I am at fault."

You will say to me that you are at fault.

Rule 2: If the reporting verb is in past tense, the tense of the reported speech will change according to the above mentioned rules.

Reporting verb said may be changed into told but there will be no 'to' if there is any indirect object after the reporting verb.

1. : He said to me," I will teach you English today."
    He told me that he would teach me English that day.
    Or He told me that he would teach me English that day.
2. : Mohan said to me," I did your job yesterday."
    Mohan told me that he had done my job previous day.
3. : Geeta said to her mother," I was using your blouse yesterday."
    Geeta told her mother that she had been using her blouse previous day.

Rule 4: the tense of the reported speech containing universal truth does not change.

"Honesty is the best policy." said the teacher to his students.

The teacher told his students that honesty is the best policy.

Rule 5: Interrogative sentences beginning with an auxiliary verb

Sub-rule (a)- the reporting verb said, told or asked or enquired change into asked or enquired and two parts of the two sentences are joined with" if", and the sign of interrogation disappear and in its place full stop is used.

Ravi said to me," Do you need my help?"

Ravi asked me if I needed his help.

"Have you seen the rainbow in the sky?'

Said the teacher to me.

The teacher asked me if I had seen the rainbow in the sky.

"Can't you do this sum." my class teacher asked me.

My class teacher asked me if I could do that sum.

"Will you accompany me this palace? "- asked the guide to me.

The guide asked me if I should accompany him to that palace.

The interrogative sentence beginning with interrogative pronouns viz – what (kya), who (kaun), when (kab), where (kahan), which (kis, kaun, kisko), whose (kiskka ya kiski), whom (kisko), how (kaise) why (kyon)

Reporting verb and reported speech will be joined by the same interrogative pronoun.

In the reported speech the verb will succeed its subject.

The interrogative sign will disappear and after the end of the sentence there will be full stop. Inverted commas will also disappear as usual.

Interrogative sentence will be changed into assertive sentences.

Examples

1. The teacher said to me," What is your name?"
    The teacher asked me what my name was.
2. The teacher said to me," Who is the Prime Minister of India?"
    The teacher asked me who the Prime Minister of India was.
3. She said to me, "What can I do for you?"
    She asked me what she could do for me.
4. He said to me, "Are you my student?"
    He asked me if I was his student.
    Reena: "Meena, what are you doing?"
    Meena: "I am studying in class ten"
    Reena asked Meena what she was doing.
    Meena replied that she was studying in class ten.
    Mother: Rohit, where did you go?"
    Rohit: Mom, I went to a friend's house."
    Mother asked Rohit where he had gone.
    Rohit replied that he had gone to a friend's house.

6. Lata: Who is your boss?"
    Mohan: He is a handsome man of 40.
    Lata asked who his boss was.
    Mohan replied that he was a handsome man of 40.
    4.- Reported speech beginning with Imperative sentence.

First of all we should understand Imperative sentence. The sentence in which request is made, order is given, asked someone not to do something, advice is given- are the Imperative sentences.

Sub -Rule (a) Reporting verb is changed according to the sense of the sentence.

(b) The sentence containing the reporting verb and that of reported speech are joined together with infinitive "to".

Examples- 1 Request: My servant said to me," Please give me one hundred rupees."

My servant requested me to give him one hundred rupees.

Forbid (Prohibition): My father said to me," Do not walk on the road."

My father forbade me to walk on the road. (When forbade is used "do not" disappear)

Or My father told me not to walk on the road.

The teacher said to the students, "Stand up on the bench."

The teacher ordered the students to stand up on the bench.

7. Mother: "Mamta, please listen to me."
   Mamta: "I am reading the newspaper and I am not free."
   Mother requested Mamta to listen to her.
   Mamta replied that she was reading the newspaper and she was not free.

8. Teacher: "Where do you want to go this summer?"
   Mohan: Sir, I want to go to Darjeeling this summer."
   Teacher asked where he wanted to go that summer.
   Mohan replied respectfully that he wanted to go to
   Darjeeling that summer.

9. Neha: 'Will you please give me some money?"
   Mother: 'How much do you need?"
   Neha requested her mother if she (mother) would give her (Neha) some money.
   Mother asked Neha how much she (Neha) needed.

10. The father said to his son, 'Don't smoke."
    The father forbade his son to smoke.

11. The girl said to me," Who are you?"
The girl asked me who I was.

12. The teacher said to his students, "The earth moves round the Sun."
The teacher told his students that the earth moves round the Sun.

13. John: How are you?'
Smith: "I am fine, thank you."
John asked Smith how he (Smith) was.
Smith replied that he (Smith) was fine and thanked him for that.

14. The teacher said to me," May God bless you!"
The teacher wished that God might bless me.

* * *

20 marks 30 minutes
Home Work: <u>Change from Direct speech to Indirect speech</u>
He said to me," Sir! How are you?"
The teacher said to the students, "Honesty is the best policy."
My father said to me," Do not tell a lie"
The servant said to his master," Please lend me one hundred rupees today."
Malti: "Do you want my help?"
Gopal: "I do not want your help now." Thank you
"Where are you living these days?" asked the teacher to me.
"What is your name?" asked the class teacher to me.
"When will you come tomorrow to my residence?" said Mrs. Khanna to me.
"Mr. Gupta, Why are you late today?" asked the boss.
The nurse said to the patient," I have already warned you to take this medicine."

Exclamatory Sentences: When the Reported Speech is an exclamatory sentence with expression of joy or sorrow or surprise, the rules for changing from Direct Speech to Indirect Speech are as follows:

Rule 1.: The reporting verb – "Say or said" will be changed into "exclaims or exclaimed as per the tense of the reporting verb.

Rule 2.: as per the sense of expression in place of say or said – exclaims or exclaimed with surprise or exclaimed with pleasure or exclaimed with sorrow will be used and exclamatory sentence will be converted into affirmative sentence in order – subject – verb – object – complement.

Example 1: My friend said, "What a beautiful scene this is!"

Indirect Speech: My friend exclaimed with surprise that that was a very beautiful scene.

Example 2: My friends said, "Hurrah! We have won the match!"

Indirect Speech: My friends exclaimed with pleasure that they had won the match.

Example 3: My friends said, "Alas! We have lost the game!"

Indirect Speech: My friends exclaimed with sorrow that they had lost the game.

As usual the sign of exclamation will disappear and full stop will be used in indirect speech.

Till now you have learnt a lot of important things about narration – expression in Direct Speech as well as in Indirect Speech within a very short period of time. Do hope it will help you in learning English language and literature. You will be able to write good English either in direct speech or in indirect speech. I am confident it will help you a lot.

*　　*　　*

E – ENGLISH GRAMMAR (VERB ONLY)

Description

Verb is one of the most important chapters of grammar. It is an essential part of sentence without which the sense or meaning of sentence remains incomplete. Every learner of English language and literature must know its definition, its kinds and its correct use. Anyone who desires to learn it can access to "Google Play" and search the related site by typing "Durga Prasad" or "Shubham Kumar" in search column.

"Description" and "About the Author" are free of access but to read the total subject one has to pay Rs.66 online.

The language in which it is written is very simple, the method that is adopted with the suitable examples is very clear and the flow that once it starts with in the beginning continues till it ends in like a fairy tale.

If we think about verb, it appears as ordinary as an earthen lamp, but it is not true. Verb is as important as heart of human beings inasmuch as in absence of the former the sentence is incomplete whereas in absence of the latter the human being is dead.

Durga Prasad
Author

*   *   *

Verb

The verb is one of the most important parts of sentence. We cannot imagine a sentence without a verb.

What is a verb?

Verb is a doing word. An action is inherent in it. It shows or indicates that an action or a work is done or executed. A verb only may be a sentence in which the subject does not come into picture inasmuch as it is quite inherent. We will have to find it out or understand what subject is hidden or inherent because as said above we cannot imagine a sentence without a subject. Subject and verb are essential parts of sentence. So far as the question of an object of a sentence is concerned it is not required at all i.e. even without an object there may be a sentence. Object may be a part or portion of sentence - may be a group or part of it as phrase or clause or something else but it is not as essential as subject and verb.

Verb is, therefore, a vital part of sentence. Similarly subject is also a vital part of sentence. Two together can make a sentence. Thus these two – one the subject and another the verb can make a sentence even without object or complement or anything else.

When we say or express something, there may not be subject in sentence. If we mark such sentences, we can find out the subject quite hidden or inherent in the sentence so expressed or spoken. For instance:

1. Stand up.
2. Get down.
3. Shut the door.
4. Do or die.

If we see all these sentences from 1 to 4, we find the verbs only, no subjects at all.

Here we can say that there is somebody in the first person to order somebody in the second person. The first person is ordering the second person something else to follow. As such "you" is inherent or hidden before each verb. In fact in such cases there is no rule to mention the subject. Now it is crystal clear that a verb is one of the most essential words/parts of a sentence. Its presence in a sentence is as necessary as blood in human body.

The definition of verb is now very clear: A verb is a word that states something about a person, a place or a thing. For example:

1. Smith plays football.
2. Patna is the capital of Bihar.
3. Water flows downward.

The verbs – "plays", "is" and "flows" say something about Smith who is a person, "is" says about Patna which is a place and "flows" says about water which is a thing.

Verb is divided in various ways based on its feature. Let us know about it one by one:

1. **Transitive Verb, Intransitive Verb and Auxiliary Verb:**

    a) **Transitive Verb: When the action of the verb passes from its subject to its object, such a verb is called Transitive Verb.** For instance:

        i) She drinks milk.
        ii) He eats bread.

    Here effect of action passes from the subjects to the objects as such the verbs "drink" and "eat" are Transitive Verbs.

2. **Intransitive Verb: When the action stops with the subject or doer or the agent, nor does it pass from the subject to its object or anybody/anything else, it is called Intransitive Verb.** For instance:

    i) She laughs.
    ii) He weeps.

    Here the effect of action remains with its agent or the doer or the subject. It does not pass to anybody or anything else.

3. **Auxiliary Verb: The verb which assists or helps to form a tense or mood of some principal verb and forgoes its own significance as**

a principal verb for that purpose is called an Auxiliary Verb. For instance:

i) She is reading a book.
ii) He has written a letter to his father.

Here "is" and "has" are the auxiliary verbs since these are assisting to form a tense or mood of the principal verbs viz. "read" and "write".

When we talk about auxiliary verb, we should also know principal or main verb. The verb that plays the main role in sentence is called main or principal verb. In another word they are not auxiliaries.

It has already been explained what an auxiliary verb is. Auxiliary verbs are only helping verbs that are used to form the tense or mood of the sentence but it is not always true inasmuch as it functions as principal or main verb also in a sentence. Let us see and compare its function in the following examples:

1. I am a farmer.
2. I am laborious.
3. I am going to market.

Here in 1 and 2 "am" is a main verb whereas in 3 "am" is an auxiliary verb helping the main verb used to form the tense of the sentence.

What I find and observe in such cases the verb even auxiliary one is followed by some noun or adjective only as in examples 1 and 2 above. When the verb is not followed by main or principal verb, though it is an auxiliary one, it functions as main or principal verb in sentence as explained in examples 1 and 2 above. When it is followed by some main or principal verb it becomes auxiliary to main or principal verb. I have made it clear so that students can understand its function as main verb as well as auxiliary verb differently in sentence.

Now let us know about Auxiliaries that can help a lot in learning English. **Auxiliaries are primarily divided into three parts:**

1. Primary Auxiliaries:

A) "Be", "am", "are", "is" in present tense and was and were in past tense.

B) "Have" and "has" in present tense and only had in past tense.

C) "Do" and "does" in present tense and only "did in" past tense.

It has already been explained that primary auxiliaries can be used as maim verb as well as auxiliary verb.

2. **Model Auxiliaries:**

A) "Can" in present tense and "could" in past tense. "May" in present tense and "might" in past tense. "Will" in future tense and "would" in past tense. "Shall" in future tense and "should" in past tense in indirect speech but when it is used – I should get up early in the morning, it is in present tense. Likewise "must" and "ought" to also come under model auxiliaries.

Model auxiliaries are used normally with main or principal verb to express different mood as order or permission, request, advice, suggestion, obligation, prohibition and so on.

B) Model verbs take no "s" or "es" in the third person singular number.

   i)   He might be present in the office.

C) Model verbs form their negative and interrogative like other auxiliaries:

   i)   I can't jump into the river.
   ii) Can you jump into the river?

D) Contracted forms of will and would are often used in spoken and in informal language as 'll and 'd:

   i)   I'd inform you if I know.
   ii) They'll come here soon.

E) The following contracted negative forms are often used and written in informal language:

   i)   Cannot = can't
   ii) Could not = couldn't
   iii) Might not = mightn't

iv) Will not = won't

v) Shall not = shan't

vi) Would not = wouldn't

vii) Shouldn't = shouldn't

viii) Must not = mustn't

F) Model verbs have no proper past tense, however could, would, might and should may be used in past tense:

    i) I could jump into this river when I was merely ten years old.

G) Model verbs have no infinitive, ing or past participle forms and cannot be followed by other model verbs:

    i) If you want to be a good student, you must be able to learn your lesson regularly.

    ii) I have been able to jump into this river since my boyhood.

3. **Semi-Models: They are called semi-models because they function partly as main verb and partly as model auxiliary.** Mainly there are three semi-model auxiliaries - dare, need and used to. For instance:

A) How dare my servant abuse me? (As a model verb in interrogative form)

B) My servant didn't dare to see me. (As a main verb)

C) Need you make a noise in the class? (As a model verb)

D) The class teacher needn't have been so cruel. (As a main verb)

E) He used to take part in games and sports. (As a main verb)

F) Do you use to walk in the morning? (As a model verb)

Now it is clear to you how one verb becomes main verb and how it becomes a semi-model auxiliary verb.

It is to be noted that most of the Transitive Verbs take a single object - I mean to say that only a single object appears normally after such a verb i.e. either a direct object or an indirect object, not both at a time.

A) He broke the glass. – The object is a noun and direct object as well.

B) Mohan killed him. – The object is a pronoun and indirect object as well.

There are some Transitive Verbs which take two objects at a time after them. These two objects are called Direct Object if they are things (not persons) and Indirect objects if they are persons (not things). For instance:

A) He gave me a pen.
B) He teaches me English.
C) He offered me some coins.
D) He asked me a question to reply.

In another way these sentences can be written, the pattern of the sentences changes but the sense or meaning remains the same.

1. He gave a pen to me.
2. He teaches English to me.
3. He offered some coins to me.
4. He asked a question from me.

In all these sentences we find two (Double) objects - one direct and another indirect.

Transitive verbs can be used intransitively in two ways:

1. When the verb is used in such a sense that no object or objects thought of using it. For instance:

A) Men eat to preserve life.
   Though "eat" is a transitive verb by nature but here it is used intransitively.
B) A newly born child can see, but a kitten is born blind. Though "see" is a transitive verb by nature but here it is used intransitively.

2. When a reflexive pronoun is omitted. For instance:

A) She drew (herself) near me.
B) Move (yourself) forward.

In these sentences "drew" and "move" are used intransitively because the reflexive pronouns – herself and yourself are omitted, so they have become intransitive.

Intransitive verbs used as transitive verbs:

3. When an intransitive verb is used in a causative sense, it becomes transitive.

A) Intransitive	B) Transitive
The horse walks.	He walks the horse.
The birds fly.	The boys fly the kites.
The girl ran down the street	The girl ran a needle into her finger.

4. Some intransitive verbs may become transitive by having a preposition added to them. For instance:

A) His friends laughed at him.
B) I wish for nothing more.
C) The police inspector asked for his name.
    Please look into the matter carefully.

In another way also verb can be divided as follows:

5. **Finite Verb – The verb which agrees with its subject in number and person, is called Finite Verb.** Such verbs tend to change their forms with the change in their subjects. For instance:

A) I am a teacher. We are teachers.
B) She is going to school. - She and her brother are going to school.
C) A boy plays football. - Boys play football.
D) She has a toy. - They have toys.
E) He writes a letter. They write letters.

In all these sentences we notice that the verb agrees with its subject in number and person.

In A) the subject "I" is the first person, singular number. As the subject changes to the first person in plural number, the verb also changes to plural number from "am" to "are. Similarly in all the examples we notice the same changes in the same order as per the rule of the grammar.

6. **Non - finite verb: Non - Finite Verb by its name is opposite to Finite Verb i.e. it retains the same form irrespective of any change in its subject in number and person.** For instance:

A) I love to sing a song when I am alone.
B) My teacher loves to sing.

We find that "to sing" retains its form even its subject changes.

I mean to say that finite verb changes in person and number of its subject but it does not happen in case of non - finite verb – non - finite verb retains its form irrespective of any change in its subject.

A sentence must have a finite verb otherwise it is not a sentence. Finite verb is a necessary part of a sentence whereas non-finite verb is not a necessary part of a sentence.

It is true that non - finite verb is an important part that expands the sense or meaning of the sentence only. Such non - finite verbs are of three types/ kinds that function as:

A) Infinitive "To"
   - to play, to walk
B) Gerund – Transitive verb + ing - playing, walking
C) Participle - playing, walking, buying
   i)   Present Participle: Going to market my son bought a bi - cycle.
   ii) Past Participle: Having gone to market my son bought a bi - cycle.

Let us see these sentences:

A) I am not able to play football as I have pain in my legs.
B) My grandfather is going to walk in the field.
C) Playing in the badminton court is prohibited.
D) Walking is a good exercise.
E) Seeing a tiger he fled away.
F) Closing his shop he went home.
G) Having seen a tiger he fled away.

H) Having closed his shop he went home.

In A and B play and walk are infinitives.

In C and D "playing" and "walking" are gerund and functions as noun.

In E and F "seeing" and "closing" are present participles whereas in G and H 'having seen' and 'having closed' are past participles.

Let us learn the structure of sentences using infinitives and gerund noun in different ways:

1. To walk is good for health.
2. To tell a lie is an offence.
3. Walking is good for health.
4. Smoking is injurious to health.
5. I like to smoke a cigarette.
6. I dislike smoking.

It shows that one sentence with infinitive may be changed into another sentence using gerund noun and it is remarkable that the sense or meaning of the sentences in both cases remains the same.

It is an art of English language and literature that we are able to express the same thought/views/ideas in a quite different way or style or order or fashion as we prefer to.

For instance:

We may express our thought in two different ways:

1. To smoke is injurious to health.
2. Smoking is injurious to health.

As infinitive plays a significant role in English language and literature, we should go into depth of its importance.

Some sentences are even without "to". In fact infinitive to is inherent or hidden in such sentences. For instance:

1. I can help you. Here infinitive 'to' is inherent in between 'can' and 'help'.

2. You should obey your teachers. Here infinitive 'to' is hidden in between 'should' and 'obey'.

3. We must pay respect to our teachers. Here infinitive 'to' is hidden in between 'must' and 'pay'.

   But there is an exception to this rule also:

   We ought to rise early in the morning. Here we cannot ignore or drop 'to' after "ought" If we do so, the sentence will be incorrect.

4. We will play football today.

5. I would like to resume my duty today.

6. He dare not say so.

7. She need not go alone.

Infinitive "to" is hidden when these transitive verbs are used as follows:

1. I made her dance.

2. He made me laugh.

3. I saw her sing.

4. We felt the earth shake.

After the subjects 'had better', 'had rather' infinitive "to" remains hidden. For instance:

A) You had better go out.

B) He had rather die than live.

Verb is also divided into:

1. **Strong Verb**
2. **Weak Verb**
3. **The Weakest Verb**

1. Strong Verbs: Strong Verbs form their past tense merely changing the inside vowel of the present tense, without having - ed, or - d or - t added to the present tense of the verb. Such verbs are called Strong Verb because they are able to make their own past tense without adding anything else.

In another way we can define Strong Verb as follows:

A verb which forms its past tense and past participle by a change in the main vowel of the present tense and without the addition of any ending like "ed", "d" and "t" is termed as a Strong Verb.

1. Write – wrote – written are in the form of present, past and past participle
2. Come – came – come are also in the same form. In these examples given above the vowel sound changes in the forms of past tense and past participle and secondly there is no ending with "ed" "d" and "t".

For instance:

Present Tense	Past Tense	Past Participle
Come	Came	come
See	Saw	seen
Write	Wrote	written
Run	Ran	run
Speak	Spoke	spoken

List of Strong Verbs that can be helpful to the learners:

	Present Tense	PastTense	Past Participle
1.	Abide	abode	abode
2.	Arise	arose	arisen
3.	Bear (bring forth)	bore	born
4.	Bear (carry)	bore	borne
5.	Beat	beat	beaten
6.	Become	became	become
7.	Beget	begot	begotten
8.	Begin	began	begun
9.	Behold	beheld	behold, beholden
10.	Bid	bade, bid	bidden, bid
11.	Bind	bound	bound, bounden
12.	Bite	bit	bitten, bit
13.	Blow	blew	blown
14.	Chide	chid	chidden, chid
15.	Choose	chose	chosen

16.	Cleave (split)	clove, cleft	cloven, cleft
17.	Cling	clung	clung
18.	Come	came	come
19.	Dig	dug	dug
20.	Draw	drew	drawn
21.	Drink	drank	drunk, drunken
22.	Drive	drove	driven
23.	Eat	ate	eaten
24.	Fall	fell	fallen
25.	Fight	fought	fought
26.	Find	found	found
27.	Fly	flew	flown
28.	Forbear	forbore	forborne
29.	Forbid	forbade	forbidden
30.	Forget	forgot	forgotten
31.	Forsake	forsook	forsaken
32.	Freeze	froze	frozen
33.	Get	got	got, gotten
34.	Give	gave	given
35.	Go	went	gone
36.	Grow	grew	grown
37	Grind	ground	ground
	Hide	hid	hid, hidden
	Hold	held	held
1.	Know	knew	known
2.	Ride	rode	ridden
3.	Ring	rang	rung
4.	Rise	rose	risen
5.	Run	ran	run
6.	See	saw	seen
7.	Shake	shook	shaken
8.	Shave	shaved	shaven
9.	Shear	sheared	shorn
10.	Shine	shone	shone
11.	Show	showed	shown
12.	Shrink	shrank	shrunk, shrunken
13.	Sing	sang	sung

14.	Sink	sank	sunk, sunken
15.	Sit	sat	sat
16.	Slay	slew	slain
17.	Slide	slid	slid
18.	Sling	slung	slung
19.	Sow	sowed	sown
20.	Speak	spoke	spoken
21.	Spin	spun, span	spun
22.	Spit	spat	spat
23.	Spring	sprang	sprung
24.	Stand	stood	stood
25.	Steal	stole	stolen
26.	Stick	stuck	stuck
27.	Sting	stung	stung
28.	Strike	struck	struck, stricken
29.	Strive	strove	striven
30.	Swear	swore	sworn
31.	Swim	swam	swum
32.	Swing	swung	swung
33.	Take	took	taken
34.	Tear	tore	torn
35.	Thrive	throve	thriven
36.	Throw	threw	thrown
37.	Tread	trod	trodden, trod
38.	Wake	woke	woken
39.	Wear	wore	worn
40.	Weave	wove	woven
41.	Win	won	won
42.	Wind	wound	wound
43.	Withdraw	withdrew	withdrawn
44.	Wring	wrung	wrung
45.	Write	wrote	written

And so on...

2. Weak Verbs:

Weak verbs are those which past tense and past participle forms are made by adding – "ed", "d" or "t". For instance:

i) Work – worked – worked

ii) Purchase – purchased – purchased

iii) Learn – learnt – learnt

In the examples given above in "I)" "ed" is added to form past tense and past participle, in ii) only "d" is added whereas in iii) "t" is added to make past tense and past participle.

Secondly in i) the vowel sound remains unchanged, the past and past participle are made by adding "ed" to the present.

In ii) Vowel sound changes and "d" is added to the present tense to make past and past participle.

Thus we can define Weak Verb which forms its past and past participle by adding "ed", "d" or "t" to the present tense either or without a change in the vowel sound is called a Weak Verb.

Present Tense	Past Tense	Past Participle
Sell	sold	sold
Bring	brought	brought
Buy	bought	bought
Teach	taught	taught
Catch	caught	caught

The following weak verbs can be helpful to the learners:

Present Tense	Past Tense	Past Participle
1. Bleed	bled	bled
2. Breed	bred	bred
3. Bring	brought	brought
4. Build	built	built
5. Burn	burnt	burnt
6. Buy	bought	bought
7. Catch	caught	caught
8. Creep	crept	crept
9. Dare	dared	dared
10. Deal	dealt	dealt
11. Dream	dreamt	dreamt
12. Dwell	dwelt	dwelt
13. Feed	fed	fed

14.	Feel	felt	felt
15.	Flee	fled	fled
16.	Hear	heard	heard
17.	Keep	kept	kept
18.	Kneel	knelt	knelt
19.	Lay	laid	laid
20.	Lead	led	led
21.	Leap	leapt	leapt
22.	Learn	learnt	learnt
23.	Leave	left	left
24.	Lend	lent	lent
25.	Light	lighted, lit	lighted, lit
26.	Lose	lost	lost
27.	Make	made	made
28.	Mean	meant	meant
29.	Meet	met	met
30.	Pay	paid	paid
31.	Rend	rent	rent
32.	Say	said	said
33.	Seek	sought	sought
34.	Sell	sold	sold
35.	Send	sent	sent
36.	Sew	sewed	sewn
37.	Shoe	shod	shod
38.	Show	showed	shown
39.	Sleep	slept	slept
40.	Smell	smelt	smelt
41.	Sow	sowed	sown
42.	Speed	sped	sped
43.	Spell	spelt	spelt
44.	Spend	spent	spent
45.	Spill	spilt	spilt
46.	Strew	strewed	strewn
47.	Sweep	swept	swept
48.	Swell	swelled	swelled, swollen
49.	Teach	taught	taught
50.	Tell	told	told

51. Think	thought	thought
52. Weep	wept	wept
53. Work	worked	worked

And so on…

3. The Weakest Verb: There is another type of verb we find in English language. It may be named as the weakest verb in the sense that the forms of such verbs neither change in the past nor in the past participle. They remain in the same forms. The list of such verbs is as follows:

	Present Tense	Past Tense	Past Participle
1.	Bet	bet	bet
2.	Bid	bid	bid
3.	Cast	cast	cast
4.	Cost	cost	cost
5.	Cut	cut	cut
6.	Hit	hit	hit
7.	Hurt	hurt	hurt
8.	Let	let	let
9.	Put	put	put
10.	Read	read	read
11.	Set	set	set
12.	Shut	shut	shut
13.	Split	split	split
14.	Spread	spread	spread
15.	Thrust	thrust	thrust
16.	Upset	upset	upset

Some of the modern grammarians have classified verbs in another type also:

1. Liking Verbs
2. Non-Liking Verbs

1. Liking Verbs: **Liking verbs have relevancy with their subjects. They indicate a specific or particular relation or connection with their subjects and as such they are called Liking Verbs.** For instance:

A) Mathew fell ill.
B) Priyanka sings loudly.
C) Milka drinks milk.
D) Virat eats bread.

In all these examples the verbs - fell, sings, drinks and eats are related or connected particularly with their subjects - Mathew, Priyanka, Milka and Virat and the effect of these verbs wholly, solely and exclusively falls on their subjects. As such these verbs are known as Liking Verbs.

2. Non-Liking Verbs: **Non-Liking Verbs are detached with their subjects, they have a particular relationship other than their subjects and as such these verbs are termed as Non-Liking Verbs. In such cases as I notice the effect of non-liking verbs normally fall on their objects.** For instance:

A) Sonali sings a song.
B) Saurabh helps me in need.
C) Kanchan is playing football.

In all these examples we don't notice any particular or specific relationship or connection of the verbs – sings, helps and playing with their subjects nor does the effect of these verbs fall on their subjects, rather their relation or connection is almost detached from their subjects. As such these are called Non-Liking Verbs.

Over and above what we have learnt till now about verbs and its different kinds or types from the different angles/characters/features we ought to know how to make verbs from adjective as well as from nouns.

1. Verbs are made from adjectives by adding prefixes or suffixes:

A) From large to enlarge
B) From fool to befool
C) From sharp to sharpen
D) From able to enable
E) From dear to endear
F) From sure to ensure
G) Pure to purify
H) Just to justify

I) Broad to broaden
J) Dark to darken
K) Haste to hasten
L) Hard to harden
M) Cheap to cheapen
N) Thick to thicken
O) Wide to widen
P) Right to rectify
Q) Clear to clarify
R) Equal to equalise
S) Special to specialise
T) Civil to civilise
U) Certain to ascertain
V) Necessary to necessitate
W) Popular to popularise
X) Regular to regularise
Y) Minimum to minimise
Z) Maximum to maximise

2. Verbs from nouns: where suffixes or prefixes are added to nouns:

A) Apology to apologise
B) Sympathy to sympathise
C) System to systematise
D) Authority to authorise
E) Character to characterise
F) Courage to encourage
G) Joy to enjoy
H) Danger to endanger
I) Power to empower
J) Office to officiate
K) Origin to originate
L) Prison to imprison
M) Blood to bleed
N) Food to feed

O) Energy to energise
P) Title to entitle
Q) Force to enforce
R) Fold to enfold

Normally verb whether it is principal or auxiliary it follows its subject but in a few cases it does not follow at all. For instance:

1. Where the sentence is an interrogative sentence, the verb precedes its subject. For instance:

A) Does he go to school?
B) Are you a teacher of this school?
C) Did your brother help you?

2. Where the sentence starts with interrogative pronouns, the verb precedes its subject.

Interrogative Pronoun is that which is used to ask a question. Such pronouns are as follows:

Where, when, which, how, what, who, whom and why – All these are used to ask questions by someone. The sentence begins with any of the interrogative pronouns the verb precedes its subject. For instance:

1. Where are you going now?
2. When will you proceed to Kolkata?
3. Which is your shirt?
4. How can you cross the river?
5. What is your aim in life?
6. Who can help you in need?
7. Whom do you want to marry?
8. Why do you want to resign from service?
    In all these sentences we notice the verbs precede their subjects and in all such cases the interrogative sentences starting with the interrogative pronouns that are used for asking questions precede their subjects.

3. Where the sentence or a part of a sentence starts with adverb, the verb precedes its subject. For example:

A) As you saw, so will you reap.
B) She doesn't know how to dance. Nor does she know how to sing.
C) My case was such that my bail petition was rejected by the court. So was yours.

4. When request is made by someone in submissive way:

A) Please lend me one thousand rupees just now. or
B) Could you lend me one thousand rupees just now, please? or
C) Would you lend me one thousand rupees just now, please?
D) This be the verse you grave for me,
E) Here he lies where he longed to be.
F) Long long ago there lived a king in Patliputra.
G) No sooner did I reach the station than the train left.
H) If I had deposited money in state bank, I would have earned compound interest.
Or Had I deposited money in state bank, I would have earned compound interest.

Verb-Subject Agreement or Subject-Verb Agreement

1. It is a general rule of the grammar that the subject must agree with its verb in number and person or vice versa. It is, therefore, a thumb rule that if the subject is plural, its verb will be also in plural. Similarly if the subject is in singular number, its subject also will be in singular number. For instance:

Table – 1

Singular number		Plural Number
1st. Person	I (am)	We (are)
2nd. Person	You (are)	You (are)
3rd. Person -	he, she, it, this (is)	They (are)
These (are)		
Those (are)		

2. A or an or one, many a, each, every, someone, somebody, anyone – all are singular numbers and as such verb after each one will be in singular numbers.

Exception to this general rule: Where verbs do not agree with their subjects:

1. **When two subjects indicate togetherness in a single symbol, the verb will be in a singular number.** For instance:

   A) The horse and cart was sold for rupees one thousand only.
   B) Bread and butter is my favourite breakfast.
   C) Two and two is four.
   D) Slow and steady wins the race.
   E) Peace and harmony keeps our mind cool.

In all these sentences from A) to F) we find the subjects in plural number but their verbs following them are in singular number.

2. **Where there are two persons but indicate one, the verb will be in singular number.** For instance:

   A) The chairman and principal has unfurled the national flag.
   B) The director and producer of this film is the same person.
   Here it is worth noting that two subjects are joined by conjunction "and" but in the former subject article "the" has been used whereas in the latter no article has been used. It is done to indicate that both are the one and the same person.

3. **Where two subjects are joined with preposition "of" the verb will follow the first one in number and person.** For instance:

   A) The quality of mangoes is good.
   B) The mangoes of this basket are rotten.

4. **When the subjects are of two nouns or pronouns are joined together with "with", "along with" and "as well as" the verbs agree with the former subject only in number and person.** For instance:

A) The class teacher as well as his students has taken part in cricket match.

B) The babies with their mother were discharged from the hospital.

C) The principal along with his teachers was present in the annual function day.

5. **When two subjects are joined with "not only ... but also" or "neither... nor" or "either... or" the verbs agree with the latter subject only in number and person.** For instance:

A) Not only the class teacher but his students also have taken part in annual function.

B) Neither you nor your sons are at fault.

C) Either you or your son is held responsible for committing this crime.

6. **When nouns denote weight, measure, amount, time, distance, the verb will be singular number.** For instance:

A) Five miles is not a long distance.

B) Two litres of milk is enough for my family.

C) Five rupees is not a big sum.

D) Two-thirds of the job is now complete.

7. **When the collective nouns are considered as one or not as one.** For instance:

A) The jury were divided in their opinions.

B) The jury has ordered to pay the fine.

8. **When the names of a country or state or institute indicate a team or group, the verb will be singular.** For instance:

A) Australia have won the world cup.

B) India have defeated South Africa by two runs.

9. **When a relative pronoun is used after its subject which is in first person or second person or third person in singular or plural number, such relative pronoun agrees with the pronoun that it follows in number and person.** For instance:

   A) I, who am your teacher, have asked you to see me on Sunday.
   B) You, who were present here, have not paid the tuition fees.

10. **After each, every, everyone, singular verb is used.** For instance:

    A) Each boy has got a prize.
    B) Every boy was present in the class.
    C) Everyone is responsible for losing the match.

11. **Some of the branches of learning look plural but in fact they are singular.** For instance:

    A) Mathematics is not an easy subject.
    B) Economics is a tough subject.
    C) Physics helps to be a space scientist.
    D) Statistics is not an easy subject.

12. **Nouns that appear as singular but in fact they are plural.** For instance:

    A) The people of our state are very educated.
    B) The sheep are always in their group.
    C) The cattle are grazing in the field.

13. **When we find more than one pronouns together as subjects connected with conjunction and the verb will be in order of 231 i.e. the second person, the first, then the third person and at last first person.** For instance:

   A) You and he were fast friends.
   B) You and I have been nominated to play together.
   C) You, he and I have got the prize.
   D) He and I were present in the meeting.

Do hope till now you have learnt a lot about verbs and their correct use in day today life.

*   *   *

E – ENGLISH GRAMMAR (ADVERB ONLY)

Description

Adverb is one of the most important parts of "Parts of Speech" of **English Grammar.** There are eight parts of speech – noun, pronoun, adjective, verb, adverb, preposition, conjunction and interjection. There is an E-Blue Book on "Parts of Speech by the author duly published in "Google Play". Anyone can read it for the sake of knowledge.

An Adverb as we take it appears to be an ordinary subject but it is not so. It is as important as any part of "Parts of Speech". An adverb is a word that modifies or describes a verb, an adverb, an adjective beside other words. In fact it heightens the state of action in an appropriate way which makes the sentence more elegant. For instance:

Monika got a prize. She went home. The reaction of getting the prize appears to be a day to day affair and as such it is an ordinary one but if we use a word how she feels after getting a prize, it expresses her feeling and here an adverb can be useful to express her feeling.

Monika got a prize.

She went home happily.

Here the word "happily" shows her feeling. How did she go home? "Happily."

The author has described the subject very broadly in a very simple language with suitable examples. **One can enrich his knowledge in a very short time particularly in leisure.**

Durga Prasad
Author

* * *

Adverb

By its name itself we can know what an adverb is. "Ad" is added to a "verb" as prefix and another word is formed as an adverb.

1. **As such we can define an adverb as a word that modifies a verb and changes the sense of the earlier sentence.** For instance:

    A) He shouts.
    B) He shouts loudly.
    C) She dances.
    D) She dances nicely.
    E) They run.
    F) They run fast.

In all the sentences of A, C and E we find the verbs after each subject but in B, D and F) we find – "loudly", nicely and fast also which modify the verbs – "shouts, dances and fast. If we question - "How does he shout?" Or "How does she dance? Or "How do they run"? The answers will be as follows:

    A) Loudly.
    B) Nicely.
    C) Fast.

Thus it is clear that an adverb is a word that modifies a verb.

2. **An adverb is a word that modifies an adverb also.** For instance:

    A) He shouts very loudly.
    B) She dances very nicely.
    C) They run very fast.

In all the sentences given above "very" is an adverb modifying its adverbs - loudly, nicely and fast.

3. **An adverb is a word that modifies an adjective.** A)She sings a very sweet song. B)Dr. Khera delivers a very good lecture.

In all these two sentences we find "very" modifying the words - "sweet" and "good" which are adjective.

4.   **An adverb is a word that modifies a pronoun also.** For instance:

A)   Almost everyone was able to cast vote this time.
       Everyone is a pronoun and almost is an adverb modifying it.

5.   **An adverb is a word that modifies a preposition.** For instance:

A)   I will be reaching home well within the stipulated time.
       "Well" is an adverb modifying the preposition "within" in A) above.

6.   **An adverb is a word that modifies a conjunction also.**

A)   I could not attend my class in time just because it was raining heavily.

7.   **Very often an adverb modifies a complete sentence.** For instance:

A)   Unfortunately I failed in the examination.
B)   Virtually we are duty bound to keep our dwelling places neat and clean.
C)   Mentally we are not ready to file a writ petition.

In a few words we can define adverb as follows:

Adverbs are such words that normally describe or modify verbs, adjectives, and other adverbs. All these verbs tell us "how", "where", "to what extent" and "why" an action is done or executed or performed.

An adverb heightens the action the ways we feel it within ourselves and express it out so that one or all to whom we speak can understand it exactly. For instance:

A)   **My friend got a prize and went home happily. Here "happily" describes the extent of action. How did my friend go home? The answer is "happily". Here we find the extent of action and realise** one's feeling exactly. **It is the quality of an adverb that enriches English language to a great extent.**

As explained above now we can summarise comprehensively what an adverb is:

A) **A verb**
B) **An adverb**
C) **An adjective**
D) **A pronoun**
E) **A preposition**
F) **A conjunction**
G) **A complete sentence**

Now you have followed how important an adverb is in English grammar and literature. Virtually everyone should learn it and should know its correct use in writing, reading and speaking. It is just like a valuable treasure that can enrich your language and literature.

Let us learn its kinds also:

1. There are mainly five kinds of adverb which are in common use in day to day life:

A) **Adverb of Time:** which denotes time or period. They are as follows: When, whenever, before, after, since, for, till, as soon as, as long as, as, while, early, late, yet, already, now, then, ago etc. All these adverbs denote the time of an action and it is known by asking a question: When? The sentences or clauses (Subordinate Adverb Clause) begin with any of these adverbs. For instance:

i) When the cat is away, the mice will play.
ii) I will repay your money whenever you come.
iii) The train had left before I reached the station.
iv) The train had left after I reached the station.
v) Since you are innocent, we will not harass you.
vi) You will be punished for you are accused of murder.
vii) I will not close my shop till you come back.

viii) As soon as I reached the station, the train left.

ix) No sooner did I reach the station than the train left.

x) The college will progress as long as you are the principal.

xi) As you saw, so will you reap.

xii) Strike the iron while it is hot.

xiii) He gets up early in the morning.

xiv) She gets up late in the morning.

xv) He is honest yet he is poor.

xvi) I have already done my homework.

xvii) Now you are free from all anxieties.

xviii) Then you will be taken to task.

xix) I saw your father two days ago.

2. **Adverb of Place:** which denotes place or position. They are as follows: Here, there, everywhere, somewhere, nowhere, near, up, down, out etc. These adverbs denote the place or position of an action and it is known by asking a question - where? The sentences or clauses (Subordinate Adverb Clause) begin with any of these adverbs. For instance:

i) Here he lies where he longed to be.

ii) Where there is a will, there is a way.

iii) You can find animals everywhere.

iv) Ice is available somewhere.

v) If you go to any planet, you will find water nowhere.

vi) The temple is near to my house.

vii) Let us go up the hill and see the sunrise.

viii) We should go down the hill for shopping.

ix) Nobody is allowed to go out of the class.

3. **Adverb of condition:** which denotes condition. They are as follows: If, unless, provided that, in case etc. These adverbs indicate the condition of an action. The sentences or clauses (Subordinate Adverb Clauses) begin with any of these adverbs. For instance:

i) If it rains, I will not go out of my house.

ii) You will get your seat provided that you come in time.

iii) You cannot secure good marks unless you work hard.

iv) In case you fail to complete the job, you will not get your wages.

4. **Adverb of Manner:** which indicates the manner of an adverb. They are as follows:

As, as if, as though etc. These adverbs indicate the manner of an action and it is known by asking a question – how? The sentence or clauses (Subordinate Adverb Clauses) begin with any of these adverbs. For example:

i) As you saw, so will you reap.

ii) He talks as if he were mad.

5. **Adverb of reason:** which indicates the reason or cause of an action and it is known by asking a question – why? The sentence or clause (Subordinate Adverb clause) begins with any of these adverbs: Because, inasmuch as, since, as etc. For instance:

i) I cannot attend my office because I suffer from fever.

ii) She cannot pay her tuition fees in time inasmuch as her father is out of station.

iii) Since he is senseless, he cannot speak.

iv) As his health is poor, he cannot take part in sports and games.

However there are some other kinds of adverb also:

1. **Adverb of effect or result:** which indicates the effect of result of an action. The sentence or clause (Subordinate Adverb Clause) begins with any of these adverbs:

So ----- that

i) My son works hard so that he can earn more.

2. **Adverb of comparison:** which indicates the comparison between one to another. For example:

i) She is taller than her elder brother.

ii)   He is so weak that he cannot walk.

iii) Cotton is not so heavy as iron.

Formation of adverbs: Every learner of adverb should also know how to form adverb words. There are mainly two methods of forming adverb words:

i) **By adding – ly as suffix to the adjective:**

    A) Easily from easy

    B) Fairly from fair

    C) Truly from true

    D) Angrily from angry

    E) Suddenly from sudden

    F) Seriously from serious

    G) Specially from special

ii) **By adding - ly as suffix to the noun:**

    A) Daily from day

    B) Weekly from week

    C) Monthly from month

    D) Yearly from year

Apart from the above there are some words which are originally adverbs:

    A) Fast – He runs fast.

    B) Direct – He says everything direct to his boss.

    C) You will be allowed to recite the poem only once.

    D) The plan is flying high.

While making adverbs from adjectives the general rules of grammar should be followed. For instance:

    A) Quick is an adjective. If we want to make an adverb, we can add "ly" unhesitatingly. The adverb word is "quickly"

    B) If we find an adjective ending in "y", then we have to change "y" into "I" and only after that we add "ly". Now the adverb is "happily".

C) If any adjective ends in "ful", one "l" that is dropped once again is added to the adjective and only "y" is added to make an adverb. In another words we can say that in such cases also as the rule given in A) above "ly" is added to the exact adjective word. For instance:

    i)   Beautifully from beautiful Carefully from careful Hopefully from hopeful

D) If any adjective ends in "l", "ly" is added to the adjective to make an adverb. For instance:

    i)   Really from real

E) If any adjective ends in "e", while adding "ly" "e" is normally dropped. For instance:

1. Truly from true
   But not in these cases:
ii) Solely from sole
iii) Wholly from whole Do hope till now everyone has learnt what an adverb is and how important it is to learn its usage in writing and speaking English.

*   *   *

E – ENGLISH GRAMMAR (PREPOSITION ONLY)

Description

Preposition is one of the most important parts of speech. It is too tough to have mastery over it. That is why most of the people ignore it.

So far as I know, I do realise that preposition is the lifeline of English Grammar and so of English language and literature to a great extent.

In view of this dexterity everyone must read it thoroughly with sheer sincerity. It will, I am sure, enrich their language and literature.

I have tried my level best to explain the chapter, though tough, with suitable examples in a very simple language so that even a beginner can understand and grasp this tough chapter with ease.

Whatever I have written about, I have written it after thorough study. It is not merely a description but a thesis with a new idea, with a unique thought and over and above with a superb presentation.

Durga Prasad
Author

*   *   *

Preposition

A preposition is a word that is normally used before a noun or a pronoun or something else to show relation of one with the other. Such relation varies time to time particularly when it is used in the beginning of a sentence or in the middle of a sentence or at the end a sentence. Whatsoever its position may be, it is true that it does show its relation with somebody or something else and this "Something else" may be any part of speech other than a noun or pronoun. It is the peculiarity of the preposition that it (peculiarity) makes it too difficult for us to understand and grasp. If it is so, nobody, as I realise, can mastery over the correct use of preposition, an error may occur any time while using it, even though carefully. The bright aspect of this subject is that the people do not mind or react on its wrong use, they take it lightly and forget it as an offence committed in ignorance. Here even "Ignorance of law is no excuse in the eye of law" does not apply at all. English is a very rich language and is spoken gently all over the world with due respect. I have a bitter experience of how the meaning or sense of a sentence changes with the use of incorrect preposition after a verb or after a noun or after an adjective in particular and after other parts of speech in general. The verb or the noun or the pronoun or the adjective remains the same but the moment a preposition changes, the sense or meaning of the sentence changes and we find one sentence is quite different from the other in sense.

So far as I know preposition is a very important part of speech. It functions to enlarge a sentence. It functions to complete an incomplete sense of a sentence. It functions to join two nouns or two pronouns or one noun and one pronoun or something in between or sometimes one alone. It is the rarest of the rare feature of the preposition that helps us in learning good English and moreover in writing good English, in speaking good English as well. The more we finish, the more we find anew to begin with.

Now we can conclude as follows:

1. **A preposition shows or indicates relation.**
    For example:

    A) There is a book on the table. (Here "**on**" shows relation between a book and the table i.e. between a noun and a noun)

B) Here is a prize for you. (Here **"for"** shows relation between a prize and me i.e. between a noun and a pronoun)

C) He jumped into the river. (Here **"into"** shows relation between jumped and the river i.e. between a verb and a noun)

D) The thief ran away quickly. (Here **"away"** shows relation between a ran and quickly i.e. between a verb and an adverb)

E) The king came with the beautiful queen. (Here shows relation between came and the beautiful i.e. a verb and an adjective)

2. **A prepositional relation may be with any part of speech.** For example:

A) I will come **in May.** (Noun)
B) This seat is reserved **for me.** (Pronoun)
C) I am tired **of working.** (Gerund)
D) She is going to market **to buy** an umbrella. (Infinitive to)
E) He succeeded **by dint of hard work.** (Phrase)
F) This is the book (**which**) you wanted to read. (Relative pronoun which inherent after the noun book)
G) I will not go out **if it rains.** (Subordinate clause)
H) Which caste do you **belong to**? (Adverbial particle)
I) **By whom** was the Ramayana written? (Passive voice)
J) **Do or die.** (Verb)
K) She came **along with** her daughter. (Preposition)
L) You are ordered to surrender **or** I will shoot you. (Conjunction)
M) **What** a beautiful scene it is! (Interjection)
N) I prefer hot tea **to cold** coffee. (Adjective)
O) The woman was crushed **under the running** train. (Participle)

3. **A preposition precedes the subordinate clause separating it from the principal clause. For example:**

A) I do not know **when his teacher comes to teach him.**
B) I do not know **where your teacher live at.**
C) I will return your book **if you see me in the library.**
D) My daughter could not attend her class **as she was sick.**
E) You cannot succeed **unless you work hard.**
F) He talks **as if he were mad.**

4. **A preposition may be phrasal. We call it a phrasal preposition also. For example:**

A) **By dint of** hard labour he stood first in his class.
B) **In spite of** a lot of obstacles she reached the height of success in life.
C) I could not attend my office **because of** fever.
D) I replied the quarries **with reference to** your letter.
E) There is a temple **in front of** my house.
F) She gave me a book **in lieu of** my pen.

5. **A preposition may be clausal. We call it a clausal preposition also. For examples:**

A) Your success depends **upon** how sincerely you work.
B) Can you believe **in** what the accused has said?
C) **Since** you a bluffer, I can't rely on you.
D) He was sentenced to death, **for** he was accused of murder.
E) No sooner did I reached the station **than** the train left.
F) **As** you sow, so will you reap.

6. **A preposition may act as an adverb while indicating time, place or position, manner, quality or quantity, extent or degree, condition, comparison or contrast and so on...**

A) When, whenever, while, till, until, before, after, for, since, as, as soon as, at, on, in, by, from, during, within, behind, towards, with, along with – all these are prepositions denoting time.
B) Where, whenever, at, on, up, down, in, out, within, under, over, above, to, into, – all these are prepositions denoting place or position.
C) At, on, by, in, with, without, through – these are prepositions indicating manner.
D) If and unless are preposition indicating condition.
E) Than, as... as, so... as are prepositions denoting comparison or contrast.

7. **A preposition may be apparent or inherent or hidden or omitted.**
   It is normally seen in case of a subordinate adjective clause particularly when a relative pronoun is the object of a preposition and also when a subordinate noun clause acts as an object. For instance:

   A) This is the book **(which)** I was looking for.
   B) The is the school **(where)** I read in.
   C) The girl **(whom)** I saw in the orchestra party is a good dancer.

8. **Some prepositions are in disguised forms. For example:**

   A) Five **o'clock** (Five of clock)
   B) **Ashore** (On shore)
   C) **Afloat** (On float)
   D) **Ablaze** (On blaze)

Kinds of preposition:

Mainly there are two types of preposition:

1. **Simple Preposition:** It is made up of a single word or is of a single syllable. For instance: in, on, out, at, up, down, above, over, for, from, to, by, under, than, since, of, off, along, but, etc.
2. **Compound Preposition:** It is made up of more than a simple preposition – more than a single syllable. When two or more than two simple or single syllable are joined together it takes the form of a compound preposition. For example: Inside, outside, within, without, upto, into, beside, around, against, amongst, behind, beneath, before, between, beyond, below, across, etc.

There are some other kinds which are named depending upon its nature of usage or function. For example:

1. **Phrasal Preposition:** We find a huge list of such phrasal prepositions in which a phase is formed with the help of one or more than one prepositions and that is why it is known as phrasal preposition. These prepositions are not alone but with a noun or a pronoun or an adjective

or a gerund or a participle etc. Such phrases are very common in use. They have enriched the English language and literature to a great extent. When we use such phrases in our writings or in our speech, its flair and flavour is multiplied and the people who read the statement or listen to the speech are impressed immensely. Everybody wants to write or speak good English but there are a few persons who deploy their head and heart in learning the art of good English. It is possible only one exerts sincerely to learn the pros and cons of each chapter of English Grammar. It is only the grammar that can teach the art and science of English language and literature. There is no other way out or a short cut to mastery over each chapter within a few days or weeks. Learning is a continuous process and the learners ought to be regular and punctual in study with sheer sincerity.

Some of the common phrasal prepositions are as follows:

Alphabetically arranged:

1. **At the top of** – at the highest – She shouted at the top of her voice for help.
2. **Because of** – owing to, on account of, due to – I could not come out of my house because of snowfall.
3. **By dint of** – by virtue of – He stood first by dint of his hard labour.
4. **By virtue of** – The tortoise won the race by virtue of steadiness.
5. For the sake of – I attend the prayer every day for the sake of mental peace and harmony.
6. **For want of** – She could not continue her study for want of money.
7. In accordance with – According to – Your pay will be fixed in accordance with the pay scales.
8. **In case of** – The farmers will get compensation in case of draught.
9. In connection with – I want to take your statement in connection with the murder case.
10. **In course of** – The matter was settled amicably in course of discussion.
11. **In favour of** – The judge delivered the judgement in favour of the innocent person.
12. **In front of** – The temple was situated in front of my house.

13. **In honour of** – A tea party was arranged in honour of the president of the club.
14. **In lieu of** – She gave me a pen in lieu of my book.
15. **In spite of** – In spite of difficulties he continued his study and succeeded in life.
16. **Instead of** – Why don't you start your own business instead of joining a private company?
17. **With an eye to** – The boy is working hard with an eye to his success.
18. **With reference to** – I have replied just now with reference to your query.
19. **In honour of** – Our College is named as M.G. College in honour of Mahatma Gandhi.
20. **In pursuance of** – I can work hard in pursuance of achieving success in life.
21. **In quest of** - Lord Buddha left the throne in quest of peace and harmony.

1. **Nouns followed by prepositions or the prepositions that follow the nouns:**
   Alphabetically arranged:

   1. Access **to** a person or thing.
   2. Accordance **with** rule.
   3. Affection **for** a person.
   4. Affinity **with** a person.
   5. Alliance **with** a person or state.
   6. Alternative **to** a plan.
   7. Ambition **for** something
   8. Anxiety **for** something.
   9. Apology **for** fault or something.
   10. Appetite **for** food.
   11. Aptitude **for** something.
   12. Arrival **at** a place **in** a country.
   13. Assault **on** a person or thing.
   14. Attachment **to** a person or a thing.
   15. Attention **to** something.
   16. Attraction **to** a thing.

17. Authority **over** a person on a subject.
18. Bargain **with** a person **for** a thing.
19. Blindness **to** one's own fault.
20. Bias **towards** a thing.
21. Care **for** safety or something.
22. Certificate **of** good conduct.
23. Cessation **from** work.
24. Charge **of** murder
25. Comparison **with** a person or a thing.
26. Complaint **against** a person for a thing.
27. Conformity **with** any one's views.
28. Consideration **for** a person of a thing.
29. Contact **with** something.
30. Contrast **to** a person or a thing.
31. Contribution **to** a fund.
32. Control **over** a person or a thing.
33. Correspondence **with** a person to a thing.
34. Craving **for** anything.
35. Conviction **of** guilt.
36. Decision **on** something
37. Degradation **from** some post or rank.
38. Dependence **on** a person or a thing.
39. Desire **for** something.
40. Deviation **from** something.
41. Doubt **about** a thing.
42. Duty **to** a person.
43. Enmity **with** a person.
44. Entrance **into** a place.
45. Escape **from** something.
46. Exception **to** some rule or regulation.
47. Excuse **for** fault or crime.
48. Exemption **from** something.
49. Experience **of** a thing.
50. Familiarity **with** a person or a thing.
51. Faith **in** a person or a thing.
52. Fine **for** a thing.
53. Fondness **of** anything.

54. Heir **to** something.
55. Identity **with** a person or a thing.
56. Immersion **into** water.
57. Inclination **to** something.
58. Indulgence **in** something, to a person.
59. Influence **over** a person.
60. Inquiry **into** a matter or case.
61. Interest **in** something.
62. Intimacy **with** a person.
63. Justification **for** something.
64. Lecture **on** a subject.
65. Look **at** a thing.
66. Lust **for** something.
67. Malice **against** a person.
68. Neglect **of** duty or work.
69. Obedience **to** something.
70. Objection **to** something.
71. Obligation **to** a person for a thing.
72. Preface **to** something.
73. Preference **to** something.
74. Prejudice **against** a thing.
75. Proficiency **in** anything.
76. Reference **to** a person or a thing.
77. Relation **of** a thing to another.
78. Reliance **on** something.
79. Reply **to** a letter or a query.
80. Resemblance **to** a person or a thing.
81. Sin **against** God.
82. Succession **to** something.
83. Supplement **to** a thing.
84. Surety **for** a person.
85. Sympathy **for** someone.
86. Title **to** something.
87. Trust **in** something.
88. Variance **with** a person.
89. Victim **to** something.
90. Victory **over** something.

91. Want **of** something.
92. Witness **to** something.

2. **Adjectives and Participles followed by Prepositions:**
Alphabetically **in** order:

1. Absorbed **in** something
2. Acceptable **to** a person.
3. Accessible **to** something.
4. Accountable **to** a person for a thing.
5. Accused **of** some charge.
6. Accustomed **to** some habits.
7. Acquainted **with** a person or thing.
8. Acquitted **of** a charge.
9. Addicted **to** bad habits.
10. Adjacent **to** a place.
11. Afraid **of** something.
12. Ambitious **of** something.
13. Amused **of** something.
14. Angry with a person **to** a thing.
15. Annoyed **with** a person at a thing.
16. Answerable **to** a person for something.
17. Apparent **to** someone.
18. Applicable **to** a case.
19. Apprised **of** a thing.
20. Apt **in** some subject.
21. Ashamed **of** some act.
22. Associated **with** a person **in** something.
23. Aware **of** something.
24. Blind **of** an eye to one's fault.
25. Close **to** a person or thing.
26. Committed **to** something.
27. Common **to** someone or something.
28. Comparable **to** something else.
29. Confident **of** something.
30. Contented **with** something.
31. Contrary **to** something.

32. Conversant **with** a person or thing.
33. Convicted **with** a charge.
34. Convinced **of** a fact.
35. Coupled **with** something.
36. Cured **of** some disease.
37. Dependent **on** a person or thing.
38. Deprived **of** something.
39. Desirous **of** something.
40. Disgusted **with** something.
41. Due **to** something.
42. Dull **of** something.
43. Eager **for** something.
44. Entangled **with** a person in a thing.
45. Entitled **to** something.
46. Envious **of** something.
47. Equal **to** something.
48. Exempted or exempt **from** something else.
49. Exhausted **with** work.
50. Exonerated **from** blame or charge.
51. Exposed **to** something.
52. Faithful **to** someone.
53. Familiar **to** something with thing.
54. Fascinated **with** a person or thing.
55. Fond **of** something.
56. Foreign **to** something.
57. Gifted **with** something.
58. Good **for** nothing.
59. Grateful **to** a person **for** something.
60. Guilty **of** charge.
61. Hungry **after** something.
62. Hopeful **of** something.
63. Identical **to** something.
64. Ignorant **of** something.
65. Immaterial **to** something.
66. Inclusive **of** something.
67. Indebted **to** a person **for** a thing.
68. Indulgent **in** some bad habits.

69. Innocent **of** charge.
70. Insensible **to** something.
71. Interested **in** a person or thing.
72. Intimate **with** a person.
73. Introduced **to** a person.
74. Involved **in** something.
75. Irrelevant **to** something.
76. Jealous **of** something.
77. Lame **of** a lag.
78. Liable **to** something.
79. Limited **to** something.
80. Lost **to** something.
81. Loyal **to** somebody or state.
82. Made **of** something.
83. Negligent **of** duty.
84. Obedient **to** somebody.
85. Obliged **to** someone for something.
86. Opposed **to** something.
87. Opposite **to** a place.
88. Overwhelmed **with** something.
89. Painful **to** one's feeling.
90. Parallel **to** something.
91. Peculiar **to** someone or something.
92. Precious **to** a person.
93. Proficient **in** some subject.
94. Profitable **to** someone.
95. Proud **of** someone.
96. Pursuant **to** an enquiry.
97. Qualified **for** something.
98. Quarrelsome **with** someone.
99. Radiant **with** smiles.
100. Reckless **of** expenses.
101. Related **to** a person.
102. Relevant **to** something.
103. Responsible **to** a person.
104. Restricted **to** something.
105. Rich **in** something.

106. Sanguine **of** something.
107. Satisfied **with** something.
108. Short **of** something.
109. Similar **to** a person or thing.
110. Sure **of** something.
111. Suspicious **of** something.
112. Tired **of** something.
113. True **to** one's words.
114. Versed **in** something.
115. Victorious **over** something.
116. Weary **of** something.
117. Welcome **to** some place.
118. Worthy **of** somebody.
119. Zealous **for** something.

3. **Verbs followed by Prepositions alphabetically arranged:**

1. Abide **by** something.
2. Abstain **from** some bad habits.
3. Accede **to** something.
4. Accuse **of** charge.
5. Adhere **to** something.
6. Agree **to** a proposal **with** a person.
7. Aim **at** something.
8. Allot **to** a person.
9. Answer **to** a person.
10. Apologise **to** a person for something.
11. Appeal **to** a person **for** something.
12. Apply **to** a person **for** a thing.
13. Apprise **of** something.
14. Argue **with** a person **for** a thing.
15. Avail **of** something.
16. Bark **at** a person or thing.
17. Bear **with** a person or a thing.
18. Begin **with** something.
19. Believe **in** somebody or thing.
20. Belong **to** a person.

21. Beware **of** someone.
22. Boast **of** something.
23. Burst **into** tears.
24. Call **on** a person.
25. Charge **with** a crime.
26. Cling **to** a person or thing.
27. Comment **on** something.
28. Complain **to** a person **for** something.
29. Comply **with** one's will.
30. Confer a thing **on** anybody.
31. Consist **of** something.
32. Convicted **with** charge.
33. Cope **with** a person.
34. Deal **with** a person **in** thing.
35. Debar **from** something.
36. Defer **to** something.
37. Depend **upon** a person or a thing.
38. Die **of** some disease.
39. Differ **with** a person **on** some matter.
40. Dispose **of** something.
41. Escape **from** somewhere.
42. Explain **to** a person.
43. Fail **in** exam etc.
44. Furnish **with** something.
45. Fill **with** something.
46. Glance **at** something.
47. Hanker **after** something.
48. Inquire **in**to a matter.
49. Insist **on** something.
50. Knock **at** the door.
51. Lead **to** something.
52. Listen **to** a person for something.
53. Look **at** something, into some matter, for something,
54. Merge **into** something.
55. Object **to** something.
56. Oblige **to** a person **for** a thing.
57. Part **with** a person or a thing.

58. Pertain **to** something.
59. Plunge **into** something.
60. Plot **against** someone.
61. Prefer **one** thing to another.
62. Preside **over** a meeting etc.
63. Prevent **from** something unusual.
64. Prohibit **from** something unusual.
65. Recover **from** illness etc.
66. Refer **to** some matter or thing.
67. Relieve **of** pain etc.
68. Rely **on** some person or thing.
69. Remind --- **of** something.
70. Revolt **against** … something.
71. Reward someone **for** something.
72. Rob someone **of** something.
73. Rule **over** a state.
74. Run **after** something, **over** an accident, **under** the wheels.
75. Sentence someone **to** some charge – punishment or fine.
76. Stare **at** a person.
77. Stick **to** something.
78. Submit **to** someone.
79. Subject **to** some condition.
80. Succumb **to** difficulties.
81. Sue **for** something.
82. Surrender **to** someone.
83. Sweep something **off** some place.
84. Sympathise **with** a person.
85. Triumph **over** something.
86. Trust **in** a person.
87. Vote **for** anything.
88. Wait **for** a person or thing.
89. Warn someone **of** something.
90. Wish **for** anything.
91. Work **at** some subject **for** something.

Note: It is suggested to get by heart all these prepositions and use them regularly.

4. **Gerund (As noun) preceded by Prepositions:**

    A) The pleader persisted **in stating** so.
    B) My teacher prohibited me **from telling** a lie.
    C) The gardener prevented me **from plucking** flowers.
    D) My mother insisted **on going** out of the house.
    E) You are debarred **from voting.**
    F) I am tired **of working** whole day.
    G) I am fond **of learning** music.
    H) I am interested **in teaching** English.
    I) He assisted me **in winning** the first prize.
    J) We should abstain **from smoking. In all these sentences from A) to J) the prepositions have preceded to the gerund (nouns.)**

5. **Sometimes Prepositions are used as infinitives and function as subject:**

    A) **To err** is human, **to forgive** is divine.
    B) **To walk** in the morning will keep you healthy.
    C) **To tell** a lie is an offence.
    D) **To help** the poor in need is a part of service.
    E) **To win** the match is our motto.
    F) **To obey** your parents should be your duty.

In all these sentences prepositions "to" is used as infinitive to and the parts of sentences are the subjects of the finite verbs in the next parts of the sentences following them.

Apart from the usage of prepositions there are some more in number which are also important to note and get by heart. However all learners should go through them carefully and note for reference and record.

Now let us know the different places of prepositions normally used in sentences:

1. **Prepositions used in the middle of sentences:**

    A) There is a laptop **on** the table.
    B) The boy jumped **into** the river.

C) She is waiting **for** the bus.

D) Please do not disturb me **at** this moment.

E) I will pay your bill **if** you come now.

F) I can sanction your loan **as** it is within my power.

The prepositions used in the sentences from A) to F) are in the middle of the sentences.

2. **Prepositions that are used in the beginning of the sentences:**

   A) **Since** it is raining, I will not go out of my house.

   B) **For** the sake of God please don't compel me to commit a crime.

   C) **In** the long run you will succeed in your life.

   D) **To** err is human, to forgive is divine.

   E) **As** you sow, so will you reap.

All the prepositions used from A) to E) are used in the beginning of the sentences.

3. **Prepositions used at the end of the sentences:**

   A) Which class do you read **in**?

   B) Which caste do you belong **to**?

   C) Which city do you live **in**?

   D) Let the counting go **on**.

   E) Which post have you applied **for**?

   F) Which subject are you interested **in**?

   G) Which milk does your baby live **on**? All the prepositions shown above from A) to G) are used at the end of the sentences. Some grammarians are of the opinion that these are not prepositions but are adverbs by nature. I agree with them to their views as these prepositions are used after verbs and also they appear apparently that they modify their adjacent verbs only.

In favour of such grammarians I would like to quote some exclusive examples:

A) Stand up.
B) Sit down.
C) Come in.
D) Get out.
E) Jump into.

All these are imperative sentences in which somebody is ordering someone to do something. At the first instance anyone can say that up, down, in, out and into are not prepositions but they are adverbial participles. If we analyse these sentence, we find some subjects are there preceding all these sentences and they are "you." You is hidden as it happens in all such cases under the grammatical rules and that is the prepositions that follow the verbs show relation to their subjects which are not apparent but in an inherent state or position. In view of this reason or ground the words used after verbs do not appear to be adverbial participles. Whatsoever the opinion or view may be on this point they are originally prepositions as do show relation between some nouns or pronouns or something else.

If we read these sentences given in serial no. 3 above carefully, we observe that all these prepositions though used after verbs do show relation with some nouns.

A) "In" shows relation to "Class" in A)
B) "To" shows relation to "Caste" in B)
C) "In" shows relation to "City" in C)
D) "On" shows relation to "Counting" in D)
E) "For" shows relation to "Post" in E)
F) "In" shows relation to "Subject" in F)
G) "On" shows relation to "Milk" in G)

So it is not correct to say that the prepositions that come in use at the end of the sentence is adverb or adverb participle.

Some of the grammarians are of the opinions that such prepositions are not prepositions but adverb participle.

But at the same time some of the grammarians having authority on grammar are of the opinion that they are originally and also by virtue of its function in a sentence prepositions though they are used at the end of a sentence succeeding a verb.

In view of the explanation with suitable reasons given above there should not be any confusion or controversy in this respect.

I have explained every important aspect logically so that the learners can understand it clearly.

Undoubtedly, preposition is known as the toughest part of speech but it does not mean it is too difficult to have mastery over it. We can learn it thoroughly provided we pay proper attention to it.

Truly speaking, sometimes I am confused with it and when I find no way out, I do consult the dictionary or the relevant books of Grammar. Nobody on this earth can challenge that he or she is versed in the subject. Every chapter of Grammar is as deep as ocean to fathom and as vast as sky to measure. Amazing! Endless too!

I can suggest to read the books, magazines, newspapers and while reading them keep a bird's eye view on use of prepositions. Gradually, you can, if not whole, be able to learn a lot.

Apart from what I have written after thorough study and research of the subject concerned, I am sure the readers will find it absolutely a new idea about, a unique thought on and a superb explanation coupled with simplicity and generosity of the language and literature of English.

Thanks!

*   *   *

E – ENGLISH GRAMMAR (CONJUNCTION ONLY)

Description

As we know there are eight parts of speech in English Grammar and one of them is conjunction which is as important as others but the tragedy is that people while reading do not pay heed to it (Conjunction) properly.

We are satisfied with the idea that conjunction is a word that joins two or more sentences or phrases or clauses but reality is something else. To know this "Something else" you will have to read it thoroughly.

The author after thorough study has described it very broadly with the suitable examples in all cases.

Durga Prasad
Author

*　*　*

Conjunction

There are eight parts of speech and conjunction is one of them. It is as important as other parts of speech.

Conjunction can be defined as a word that is used to join two or more than two words or clauses or sentences. For instance:

A) I bought a shirt and a pant for my son. "**And**" joins two words – a shirt and a pant. "**And**" is a conjunction.

B) You may like to purchase a cow and calf or a horse and cart. "**Or**" joins two phrases i) - A cow and calf and ii) a horse and cart. "**Or**" is a Conjunction.

C) This is the book which I bought today. "**Which**" is the conjunction that joins two clauses - i) This is the book. - Independent Clause and ii) Which I bought today - Dependent Clause. "**Which**" is a conjunction.

D) Mohan is poor but Sohan is rich. "**But**" joins two sentences i) Mohan is poor. ii) Sohan is rich. "**But**" is a conjunction.

One word may be a conjunction or may be an adverb or may be a preposition. It depends upon how and where it is being used in a sentence. For instance:

A) **Before**

   a) I have never visited this city **before**. (Before is an adverb here.)

   b) The accused appeared **before** the judge. (Before is a preposition here)

   c) The thieves fled away **before** I entered my house. (Here before is a conjunction)

B) **For**

   a) What are you looking **for**? (For is an adverb here)

   b) The pleader waited **for** the client. (For is a preposition here)

   c) I could not attend my office, **for** I was seriously ill. (Here for is a conjunction)

C) **Since**

    a) I have never seen **since**. (Here it is an adverb)

    b) It has been raining **since** last Monday. (Here it is a preposition)

    c) The student was punished **since** he was found smoking in the class. (Here it is a conjunction)

D) **On**

    a) Let the counting go **on**. (Here on is an adverb)

    b) The book is **on** the table. (Here on is a preposition)

    c) Your success depends **on** how hard you work. (Here on is a conjunction)

E) **After**

    a) The driver came soon **after**. (Here after is an adverb.)

    b) He resumed his duty **after** a weak. (Here after is a preposition)

    c) The train started **after** I reached the station. (Here after is a conjunction.

F) **In**

    a) Please come **in**. (Here in is an adverb)

    b) She is reading **in** her bed room. (Here in is a preposition)

    c) The judge did not believe **in** what the accused said in his defence. (Here in is a conjunction)

The function of conjunction is summarized as follows:

A) It **joins** either two words or two sentences irrespective of anything else.

B) It is either **coordinates or subordinates**.

C) It is **not connected** with any object as a preposition.

D) Nor **does it qualify or modify** any word that an adverb does.

E) It may be used normally **in between** or **in the beginning** or **at the end** of a sentence with the very purpose of joining or connecting or coordinating or subordinating in any way that deems necessary.

It is a very unique as well as interesting feature or characteristic of conjunction and every learner of Grammar ought to study it attentively.

There is always criticism or confusion or controversy or contradiction for the right or wrong use and argument for and against that is made but the very truth in explaining the subject in question with sheer sincerity comes up as a winning wizard and the rest is left behind as hush.

Kinds of Conjunction:
Mainly there are only two types of Conjunction:

1. **Co-ordinating and**
2. **Subordinating**

A word that is used to join two or more simple sentences is called a coordinating conjunction. Coordinating because one simple sentence coordinates to the other simple sentence in getting together i.e. becoming one sentence without changing the sense or meaning that each has had earlier. Such conjunctions are as follows:

i) **And:** It is one of the most common conjunctions. When we think of a conjunction, it starts striking our mind as the best example and this word comes out of our mouth all of a sudden. For instance:

a) Mathew is going to school. Ruby is coming from school.
   Mathew is going to school and Ruby is coming from school.
b) She is laborious. I am laborious too.
   She is laborious and I am laborious too.
c) Please come in. Please sit down.
   Please come in and sit down.
d) Thomas is my brother. Ruby is my sister.
   Thomas is my brother and Ruby is my sister.

ii) **For:** It is also an important conjunction used by us off and on.

a) He could not buy a mobile hand set. He was too poor.
   He could not buy a mobile hand set, for he was too poor.

b) Rohit was punished by his teacher. He had stolen a pen.
Rohit was punished by his teacher, for he had stolen a pen.

iii) **But:** But is used in the middle to connect and show the relation between the two sentences that are equally important.

a) The watchman is poor. He is honest.
The watchman is poor but he is honest. Or the watchman is poor but honest.

b) Rosy worked hard. She failed in the examination.
Rosy worked hard but she failed in the examination. Or Rosy worked hard but failed in the examination.

iv) **Yet:** Yet is rarely used by us. Somehow or other it is synonymous to but to some extent and as such people avoid to use it. We should use it suitably wherever necessary.

a) My elder brother is an officer. He gets handsome salary. He is not satisfied.
My elder brother, an officer, gets handsome salary, yet he is not satisfied.

b) The boy is lean and thin. He can fight with anybody.
The boy is lean and thin, yet he can fight with anybody.

v) **Or:** It is commonly used by us particularly when we talk to each other.

a) Do your duty. You may go home.
Do your duty or you may go home.

b) You can argue yourself. You can authorise your pleader to represent.

You can argue yourself or you can authorise your pleader to represent.

Again Coordinating Conjunction is divided into four parts according to feature. They are as follows:

A) **Cumulative:** When one statement or fact is added to another it is known as cumulative coordinating conjunction. For example:

And: One was jailed and the other was acquitted.

Both ... and: The accused was both imprisoned and fined.

Also: He is a fool and you also.

Too: He was a gambler and a drunkard too.

As well as: You as well as your son is dishonest.

No less than: I am no less grateful to you than your father.

Not only ... but also: He was not only a cheat but a bluffer also.

B) **Adversative:** It means one statement or fact is contrasted with against another. For example:

But: He is disappointed but courageous.

Still: You are wealthy, still you are not happy.

Yet: He is very rich, yet he is not contented.

However: You criticize me, you are, however, my fast friend.

Whereas: You take care of your wealth whereas I take care of my health.

While: She was working while her sister was sitting idle.

Only: Attend the party, but do not stay longer.

Lest: Walk carefully lest you should stumble.

C) **Alternative:** It is just opposite to one another. There is an option or choice in between the two statements or facts – one can chose either of the two.

For example:

Either ... or: Either he has stolen my ring or his younger brother.

Neither ... nor: Neither you are guilty nor your sister. She neither danced nor sang a song. He was neither punished nor fined.

Otherwise: Be a good citizen, otherwise you will have to repent.

Else: Do not pluck flowers, else you will be beaten.

Or: Follow the traffic rules, or pay the fine.

D) **Illative:** When one statement or fact is inferred or proved by another, it is said to be illative coordinating conjunction. For example:

Therefore: The accused was found guilty of murder and therefore he was sentenced to death.

Then: Tell the truth, then you will be acquitted.

So: He did not obey his master, so he was dismissed from service.

So then: It is the right time to go, so then let us proceed.
For: He did not turn up, for he was sick.

But one important thing must be kept in mind that coordinating conjunctions are normally used in the middle of two sentences if we go by its definition and its feature "Joins." but in a very few cases it is used in the beginning of subordinate adverb and subordinate noun clause too. The unbelievable peculiarity of conjunction is that sometimes it does not join any sentence rather remains intact in between the part of independent (principal or main clause). It will be discussed and properly explained in latter stages.

1. **Subordinating Conjunction:** These conjunctions are related absolutely to **subordinate clause:** Subordinate noun clause or subordinate adjective clause or subordinate adverb clause and always come before the subordinate or dependent clause. In another words we can say that subordinate clause begins with such subordinating conjunctions only. For example:

    a) This is the book. I bought today.
    b) This is the book **which** I bought today.
        Here **"which"** is a subordinating conjunction.

I do not know **when** the train arrives.
I will not go out of my house **as** it is raining.
Here **"when"** and **"as"** are the subordinating conjunctions.
There are three types of Subordinate Clause which begin with subordinating conjunctions:

1. **Subordinate Noun Clause:** Here a noun clause functions as follows:

A) **Object to the verb of the Independent Clause. For example:**

    i)   I know **why** he is sad today.
    ii) I did not hear **what** he said to me.
    Here **"why"** and **"what"** are the subordinating conjunctions object to the verbs "Know" in i) and "Hear" in ii)

B) **Object to the preposition. For example:**

    i)   Your success depends **upon** how you work.

    ii)   I do not believe **in** what he has said.

Here **"how"** and **"what"** are the subordinating conjunctions object to the prepositions "Upon" in i) and "In" in ii)

C) **Complement to a verb. For example:**

    i)   This is exactly **what** I wanted from you.

    ii)   My question is **whether** he was present at the spot of occurrence.

    iii) It is **where** my parents liked to settle in.

Here **"what"**, **"whether"** and **"where"** are the subordinating conjunctions.

2. **Subordinate Adjective Clause. For example:**

    i)   This is the book **which** I bought today.

    ii)   This is the house **where** my parents live in.

    iii) This is the right time **when** you can start your business.

    iv) That was the reason **that** we lost the case.

    v)   He is the boy **who** has stolen my camera.

    vi) Can you recognise the boy **whom** we met yesterday?

          Here "which", "where", "when", "that", "who" and "whom" are the subordinating conjunctions.

3. **Subordinate Adverb Clause. For example:**

All Subordinate Adverb Clauses either precede or succeed the Independent clauses beginning with Subordinating Conjunctions modifying or describing the place, time, cause or reason, result, purpose, manner, comparison, contrast, condition etc. For example:

    i)   You will be punished **if** you abuse anyone.

    ii)   You will not be paid full wages **unless** you finish the work.

          Here **"if"** and **"unless"** are the subordinating conjunctions.

Some of the Subordinating Conjunctions are noted below for the sake of knowledge:

i)   Place – **where, while, whenever**
ii) Time - **When, whenever**
iii) Cause or reason – **since, because, as, inasmuch as**
iv) Result – **That, So that**
v)   Purpose – **That, so that, in order that**
vi) Manner – **As if, as though, as**
vii) Comparison – **Than, as ... as, so ... as**
viii) Contrast – **Even if, though, even though**
ix) Condition – **Unless, until, if**

All the conjunctions shown in the bold letters from serial no i) to ix) are Subordinating Conjunctions.

A few examples are given below so that the learners can understand and grasp easily:

i)   Your sister is taller **than** you.
ii)   You are not **as** tall **as** your sister is.
iii) Do not go out of the house **as** it is raining.
iv)   I will not leave the cabin **unless** you come back.
v)   He talks **as if** he were mad.
vi)   Work hard **so that** you can be successful in business.
vii) I could not attend the meeting **since** I was out of station.
viii) My servant was absent **because** he was suffering from fever.
ix)   You can do **as** you like.
x)   I will repay your money **whenever** you come.
xi)   Work sincerely **while** you are on duty.
xii) The old man is **so** weak that he cannot walk.
xiii) He can help you **even if** he is poor.
xiv) He was expelled from the examination, **for** he was found using unfair means.
xv)   I never mind **if** you go against me.
xvi) Walk carefully **lest** you should stumble.
xvii) I am not economically sound **yet** I will pay your consultation fees.

Here all the words shown in the **bold letters** are subordinating conjunctions. It may please be noted that every learner should understand and use these conjunctions in the sentences he/she writes or speaks in everyday life. But one important thing must be kept in mind that coordinating conjunctions are normally used in the middle of two sentences if we go by its definition and its feature "Joins." but in a very few cases it is used in the beginning of subordinate adverb clause and subordinate noun clause. The unbelievable peculiarity of conjunction is that sometimes it does not join any sentence rather remains intact in between the part of independent (principal or main clause).

So far as I have studied, have observed and have come to a conclusion in the context of what I have pointed it out above, the very purpose of conjunction is served when it is used before a subordinate or dependent clause irrespective of its place in a complex sentence in which at least there is an independent (principal or main) clause or succeeding or preceding or in the middle of it there is another dependent (subordinate) clause. **For example:**

1. The rules as followed in case of coordinating conjunctions are now followed in case of subordinating conjunctions also:

    A) I will not go out of my house **if** it rains. (if is in the middle)
    B) He was sentenced to death **because** he had murdered his wife. (because in the middle)
    C) I do not know **where** he lives at. (where is in the middle)
    D) It is not true **what** he has said. (what is in the middle)
        In all these above sentences of complex nature we find two clauses one independent and the other dependent and these two clauses are joined by some conjunctions viz. if, because and where. The conjunctions here function mainly to join or connect two clauses and its function is under the purview of the related rules.

2. Now let us see and observe these complex sentences comprising of at least one independent clause and other dependent clause:

    A) **If** it rains, I will not go out of my house. (**if** is in the beginning)
    B) **When** the cat is away, the mice will play. (**when** is in the beginning)
    C) **Where** there is a will, there is a way. (**where** is in the beginning)
    D) **What** he has said is not true. (**what** is in the beginning)

E) **Since** you are my servant, you are just like a member of my family. (since is in the beginning)

F) **As** you sow, so will you reap. (as in the beginning)

In all these above sentences of complex form we notice and observe that there are two clauses in each sentence – one dependent clause in the beginning and another independent clause just after that. All the conjunctions such as if, when, where, what and as do not join any sentence or clause and under the purview of the rules these should not be conjunctions as they do not join or connect at least two sentences or clauses or phrases but even then they are conjunctions by nature or as all these behave as conjunctions. If we omit them from the complex sentence, its sense will become incomplete, it will remain no longer a sentence. It is the conjunction in each case that helps join these two clauses and thus makes it meaningful.

It is, therefore, concluded without any reason or doubt that all these words used as subordinating conjunctions shown above are conjunctions

In nature.

3. Now let us see and observe the following complex sentences comprising of one independent clause and other dependent clause when the subordinate clause, preceded by subordinating conjunction, is **in between the parts** of the independent clause:

A) The school (**where**) I read in is far away from my house.

B) The book (**which**) you have given me is very useful.

C) The time **when** the train arrives at the platform is not certain.

D) The reason **why** she is sad is not known to me.

E) The process **how** sugar is prepared is known to the chemist only.

F) The boy **whom** I saw at the bar house appears to be a criminal.

G) All **that** glitters is not gold.

H) He **that** is down needs fear no fall.

I) All is well **that** ends well.

If we analyse the above complex sentences, we observe that all the subordinate clauses are in between the parts of the independent clauses beginning with the subordinating conjunctions as usual.

A) I) Where I read in ii) "The school" one part and "is far away from my house" is another part of the independent clause and both make a complete sentence. Similarly it so happens in all other sentences from B to H.
B) "Which you have given me" and "the book is very useful".
C) "When the train arrives at the platform" and "the time is not certain".
D) "Why she is sad" and "the reason is not known to me".
E) "How sugar is prepared" and "the process is known to the chemist only".
F) "Whom I saw at the bar house" and "the boy appears to be a criminal".
G) "That glitters" and "all is not gold".
H) "That is down" and "he needs fear no fall".
I) "That ends well" and "all is well".

The first clause is dependent whereas the second is quite independent. As stated and explained above the dependent clauses are in between the parts of the independent clauses. As soon as these parts wisely separating the dependent clauses from within the independent clauses, are joined together they become independent clauses with complete sense.

All these words as used and shown above are subordinating conjunctions by nature and under the purview of the definition as well as by its function as does in the sentences duly cited as examples above.

There is no exaggeration to say that a new idea, a unique thought and a logical explanation will be fruitful to one and all who are interested in learning this smaller chapter in a broader way or sense in order to enrich their English language and literature in the right perspective.

* * *

E – ENGLISH GRAMMAR (INTERJECTION ONLY)

Description

Out of the eight parts of speech in English Grammar Interjection is the last one.

As it appears so short, it does not draw much of our attention and that is why we normally ignore it.

But in fact, it is no less important than any other parts of speech.

The author after thorough study has described it broadly with suitable examples. Its explanation is quite logical, its approach is quite superb and its description is quite unique.

It is no exaggeration to say that it is a research paper on "Interjection."

Durga Prasad
Author

*　　*　　*

Interjection

An interjection is the last part of speech after conjunction. It is also as important as other parts of speech in English grammar but J.C. Nesfield, a veteran grammarian says that an interjection is not a Part of Speech, since it has no grammatical connection with any word or words in a sentence. According to him, an interjection is merely an exclamatory sound, thrown into a sentence to denote some strong feeling or emotion.

Truly speaking the explanation that is made by the great grammarian appears to be logical as it is rarely used by people while writing or speaking English. However its importance comes up and realized by us when anything abnormal happens before our eyes and the effect of such happening strikes our mind all of a sudden, the feeling or emotion bursts into some sort of exclamation out of our mouth. **Such a sudden exclamation is known as an interjection in English grammar.** The very purpose of teaching it to the learners is to apprise them actually of what types of word or words are expressed all of a sudden on different occasions arising out of different types of feelings which are related to joy (pleasure), grief (sorrow), amusement, greeting (welcoming), approval (appreciation), attention, hatred etc.

Thus, an interjection is a word that expresses some reaction of our mind as and when we feel to see or hear some unusual things all of a sudden. It is the sudden result or reaction stimulated arising out of emotion.

It is to be noted that an exclamatory sign (!) is also used just after such word.

Each feeing or emotion has a specific exclamatory word/words that are commonly used by us:

1. Joy or pleasure – **Hurrah!, Hip! Hip! Hurrah!**
2. Grief or sorrow – **Oh!, ah!, alas!**
3. Amusement – **Ha! Ha!** (Here two words)
4. Greeting or welcoming – **Hello!**
5. Approval or appreciation – **Bravo!**
6. Attention – **Lo!, hush!**
7. Surprise or delight – **Wow!, what!**
8. Hatred – **Fie! Fie!** (Here two words)
9. Hint or indication - **Ho!**

The sentence beginning with such an interjectional word or so-called exclamatory word is complete in a sense only when it is followed by an exclamatory sentence. In place of full stop a sign of exclamation (!) is used as per the rules of grammar. For instance:

1. It is a very beautiful scene. It is an assertive sentence. Its sense is complete. Hence, a full stop (.) is used at the end of the sentence.
2. What a beautiful scene it is! It is an exclamatory sentence. Its sense is complete. Hence, an exclamatory sign (!) is used at the end of the sentence instead of a full stop.

There should not be any confusion about the use of the exclamatory sign. An exclamatory sign is used after each such word and another exclamatory sign is used after the end of the exclamatory sentence. For example:

1. **Hurrah! We have won the match!**
2. **Alas! We have lost the game!**
3. **Ha! Ha! The tortoise reached the destination earlier!**
4. **Hello! You are welcome to my new house!**
5. **Bravo! Australia won the final cricket match!**
6. **Lo! The parachutes jumped from the airplane!**
7. **Hush! The snake is entering your drawing room!**
8. **Wow! How dreadful is the cobra!**
9. **What a beautiful scene!**
10. **Fie! Fie! How she killed her own baby!**
11. **Ho! What a dangerous bull behind you!**

Apart from what has been stated above about interjection, there is the certain mood of parts of speech particularly noun, pronoun, verb, adverb, preposition, conjunction, interjection and a few others which can be used in an interjectional as well as in an exclamatory sense. It will add to the treasure of knowledge of learners so far as this particular chapter of interjection is concerned.

Let us read the examples carefully and understand the mood of the sense in interjection as well as in exclamation.

1. **Noun – A great fool! Foolish fellow! Dreadful sight! Dangerous weapon!**
2. **Pronoun – What a sad affair it is! What a beautiful scene it is! What an amazing win it was! What a wonderful man he is!**
3. **Adjective – Shocking! (Here noun news is inherent), Amazing! (Here some noun like play or win or something understood), Wonderful!**
4. **Verb – Drowning! Burning! Falling! (Here some action going on all of a sudden)**
5. **Adverb – How very grateful to you! Why extremely annoyed! (Here somebody understood)**
6. **Preposition – Of what avail! (Here something understood)**
7. **Conjunction – If I were a multimillionaire! If I could see her once again!**
8. **Interjection or exclamation – What a dreadful night! Alas! We lost the match! What nonsense!**

Apart from the part of speech, there are some other parts of grammar that can be used as an interjection or exclamation.

1. **Infinitive – To think that he should have died!**
2. **Gerund Noun – Going back is cowardice!, Surrendering is death alike!**
3. **Imperative – Hear! Hear!, Do or die! Stand up! Get out! Go to hell!**

Sometimes in the extreme effect of sudden emotion or stimulation or mood, while expressing the feeling inside within the heart or mind, only the main verb is spoken out and the auxiliary verb with its subject is left out – the speaker understands what he means to say and the listener also tries to follow it.

1. **Why wait for a longer period! Why not kill him now! Why leave her for ever! How to believe in him!**
   It is notable that a single word can be an interjection. For example, a) Nonsense! b) Idiot! c) Wonderful! d) Amazing!

The meaning of each interjection is understood.

It means somebody or something is nonsense or idiot or wonderful or amazing. Two or more than two words also act as an interjection. A group of words denoting complete or incomplete sense can be an interjection.

2. **Two words can be an interjection. For example:**
   a) How dreadful! b) So dangerous!

3. **More than two words can be an interjection. For example:**
   If I were a king!, A great foolish! A nonsense argument! A false statement! A bundle of lies!

A group of words with incomplete sense can be an interjection. For example:

4. **How very grateful to you! What a dreadful night!**
   All these exclamatory sentences have no subjects of their own as such they are not considered as a complete sentence. It is true that their subjects are inherent or understood.
   We can transform them into assertive sentence also.

A group of words having complete sense can be an interjection. We do call it an exclamatory sentence also. For example:

5. **What a sad affair it is!, What a beautiful scene it is!**
   All these two exclamatory sentences are complete in a sense since they have a subject and finite verb of their own.

What a sad affair it is! It means – It is a very sad affair.
What a beautiful scene it is! It means – It is a very beautiful scene. English language and literature are so flexible that even the least words are allowed to use particularly in spoken English. The people listen to the speech and understand what is spoken or expressed. It is traditionally acceptable to one and all. Moreover the feeling that is described so shortly multiplies the beauty of language and literature of English to a great extent.
That is why English is recognized as an international language all over the world.

* * *

E – ENGLISH GRAMMAR (PUNCTUATION ONLY)

Description

The word punctuation is derived from the word "To punctuate" which is a finite verb. To punctuate means is to mark some specific sign after a word, in between words, both sides of words and after the end of a phrase, a clause or a sentence. It is just like a pause – shorter or longer that the speaker stops while speaking anything after a certain word or a group of words or phrase or clause or sentence so that the listeners can follow him or her with ease.

To know more about it one has to read whole description explained elaborately with suitable examples.

Durga Prasad
Author

*　　*　　*

Punctuation

Grammar is divided into five important parts which are as follows:

1. **Orthography:** By which children from 3 to 5 years of age learn alphabets i.e. A to Z – capital and small letters both – recognising each letter, then reading and at last writing them properly and nicely. It is the primary stage of learning English particularly when the children are of merely 3 to 4 years of age. Initially the children are taught at home by their parents to repeat these letters one by one from A to Z. The mother plays a vital role here as she is almost all the time associated with their babies. With the pace of time the baby grows and starts uttering a few words in their own broken piece of words which their parents follow what they mean to say.

    Later on they are admitted to Montessori schools to learn the lessons properly in a group of similar age from their class teachers. It is the very critical period of children when they need proper nourishment and utmost care besides teaching inasmuch as they are too unable to express actually what they need time to time during the period of their stay in schools.

2. **Etymology:** It is another important division of grammar where word formation with the help of letters is taught to the students by their teachers.

3. **Syntax:** The students are taught how to make and write sentences - at first short and simple sentences and later on long as well as compound, mixed and complex sentences.

4. **Punctuation:** Punctuation teaches us to use some specific mark/marks after words, in between words, both sides of words and lastly at the end of sentence.

    Such marks are used necessarily while writing anything as a sort of sentence or passage in order that the readers can understand thoroughly what the writers want to say or express. Secondly it determines the exact pause - short or long, exact accent or stress while writing any passage or script or statement and so on.

5. **Prosody:** It is all about poetry, all about the method or process of composing poems properly under the specific rules of grammar. It is

a subject that is prescribed for very higher classes i.e. in honours and master degree of English language and literature in syllabus.

The chapter that I want to teach here is related to punctuation. Punctuation is prescribed in the syllabus for the students of secondary and higher secondary classes as such it is necessary for them to learn this chapter attentively.

Punctuation

The word punctuation is derived from the word "To punctuate" which is a finite verb. It means to mark some specific sign after a word, in between words, both sides of words and after the end of a phrase, a clause or a sentence. It is just like a pause – shorter or longer that the writer or speaker stops while writing or speaking anything after a certain word or a group of words or a phrase or a clause or a sentence so that the readers or listeners can follow him or her with ease. Thus punctuation carries the same sense or meaning in the right perspective as it throws light upon on the method or procedure as to how correctly it is used when we write anything or even speak anything in course of our examination, business or trade or commerce or speech. It is a nothing but a specific mark – short or long, interrogatory or exclamatory which is put or placed after a word or a clause or a sentence, in between two words, both sides of words and at the end of a phrase or a clause or a sentence.

The very purpose of using punctuation is to facilitate the readers to follow and understand what the writers actually want or desire to express.

If it is not used rightly at its right place, it is no exaggeration to say that the heaven may fall, anything may happen, an accused may be acquitted and an innocent may be punished and so on...

Punctuation and its right use at the right place ought to be taken care of while drafting an agreement or contract or report, sanctioning or approving some proposals or estimates or budgets or delivering order or judgement.

From this point of view one can understand its importance in our day to day life irrespective of our nature of job or work or involvement in study as students or researchers, workmen or professionals.

The important marks of punctuation are as follows:

1. Full stop:

A) It is used when the statement is complete. After every sentence except interrogative and exclamatory ones a full stop is used. For instance:

a) Sit down.
b) Please come here.
c) Do not shout.
d) He is going to school.
e) I have done my work.
f) All that glitters is not gold.
g) Two and two is four.
h) The journey of a thousand miles begins with a single step.
i) Honesty is the best policy.
j) Rome was not built in a day.
k) Labour never goes in vain.
l) Mohan is poor but honest.
m) Going to market she bought an umbrella.
n) I do not know when he will come back.
o) What he said is not true.
p) When the cat is away, the mice will play.
q) The news that the old man died of diarrhoea is true.
r) He is too weak to walk.
s) The teacher said to us, "The earth moves round the Sun."
t) Iron is heavier than cotton.
u) Man can be defeated but cannot be destroyed.
v) Love is just like the colourful wings of a butterfly.
w) Time and tide waits for no man.
x) Courtesy begets courtesy.
y) Man is the master of his own destiny.
z) Impossibility is found in fool's dictionary.

The sentences given above from a) to z) are of different kinds – simple, compound and moreover complex as per the form and at the same time affirmative, negative and imperative as per the sense. After every sentence a full stop has been used since the sense or meaning is complete in all respect.

B) It is used after abbreviation:

a) B.A. for Bachelor of Arts
b) M.A. for Master of Arts
c) M.L.A. for Member of Legislative Assembly
d) M.P. for Member of Parliament

Now with the use of IT devices such full stops are either omitted or ignored. People simply write MP, MLA and so on…

C) Where no full stop is used:

i) **After those abbreviations which are formed with the first and the last letter of a specific word:**

a) Dr M.K. Saha
b) Mr B.K. Agarwal
c) St Mother Teresa

ii) **After abbreviations relating to denote weights and measures:**

a) hr for an hour
b) kph for kilometre per hour
c) rpm for running round per minute
d) kg for kilogram
e) mm for millimetre
f) mg for milligram

iii) **No full stop is used after any letter forming an acronym that is pronounced as a single word:**

a) GATE for Graduate Aptitude Test For Engineers
b) CAT for Common Admission Test
c) WHO for World Health Organisation

iv) **No full stop is used after such an abbreviation formed ignoring some letters succeeding to it:**

    a)   Math for mathematics
    b)   Ad for advertisement
    c)   Psycho for Psychology
    d)   Bio for Biology.
    e)   Exam for Examination

v) **No full stop is used after the names of persons in a shortened form. Moreover these letters are joined together also.**

    a)   ML Sharma for Mohan Lal Sharma.
    b)   SK Singh
    c)   RK Sinha
    d)   Dr APJ Abdul Kalam
    e)   MS Dhoni

Earlier a full stop was used after such a letter but with the development of IT devices it is not used.

Whereas its use is now mandatory after such abbreviations:

    a)   MBBS or M.B.B.S. (Bachelor of Medicine and Surgery)
    b)   MS or M.S. (Master of Science or Master of Surgery)
    c)   MBA or M.B.A. (Master of Business Administration)

With the development of science and information technology all around the world dot (.) is used as identity of Email and Password of a person and dot (.) which resembles to Full Stop is widely used in order to distinguish one to another for the users in billions. It is the dot that helps distinguish one from the other to a great extent. For instance:

www.e-bluebooks.com

Durga.prasad.1946@gmail.com

In Computer Science & Technology and Information Technology it is termed as dot (.). In fact, dot is nothing but a full stop. Millions and millions of the people all over the world have their own identity of Email and Password which must differ from one another. When one identity proposed tallies with the other already in existence, it is discarded or ignored. Then this dot helps a lot. People use the dot after his or her name or surname etc. in order to be a new one and when it doesn't tally with anyone already in use, it is accepted.

2. Comma:

Normally we remember comma (,) after full stop (.) how and where it is to be used in the sentence we write in our day to day work.

I like to teach through examples as it would be easier to understand.

i) **If more than two words come one after another, a comma is used after each word but not after the last one succeeded by conjunction "And." For example:**

A) Phillips, Mathew, Thomas and George are the students of our school.
B) Worry, curry and hurry can spoil your life.

ii) **A comma is used to separate a phrase in relation to the same person, place or thing:**

A) My uncle, the principal of my school, presided over the meeting yesterday.
B) Miss Rosy, a student of our college, was selected to represent our college in chess competition.

iii) **A comma is used to separate a question tag:**

A) It is a fact, isn't it?
B) You are a boxer, aren't you?

iv) **If anyone replies yes or no in reply to a question, a comma is used after yes or no:**

A) Question: Can you jump into the river?
Reply: Yes, I can jump into the river. Or
Yes, I can.

B) Question: Can you drive a car?
  Reply: No, I cannot drive a car. Or
  No, I can't.

v) **When an adverb at the beginning of a sentence modifies the whole sentence:**

A) Unfortunately, he was not selected for the post applied for.
B) Obviously, you will have to follow the traffic rules while driving a car.

Note: But now people use such adverbs straightway omitting or ignoring it (a comma) for their convenience.

vi) **In case a word or a group of words or a phrase or a clause is used just after an auxiliary verb or a subject or a subject alike, a comma is used after that:**

A) I, therefore, request you to sanction my loan.
B) It is, in my opinion, the best policy to settle the issue.

vii) **When a subordinate adverb clause precedes or succeeds an independent clause, a comma is used to separate one from the other:**

A) When precedes:
  a) When the cat is away, the mice will play.
  b) Where there is a will, there is a way.

B) When succeeds:
  a) I will not go out, if it rains.
  b) I cannot resume my duty, because I am confined to bed.

viii) **A comma is used after the reporting verb to separate it from the reported speech:**

A) My teacher said, "The earth moves round the Sun."
B) She said to me, "Can you teach me English?"

ix) **A comma is used between nouns or pronouns in apposition:**

    A) Akbar, the son of Hunmayu, ruled India for more than fifty years.

    B) Mr CP Phillips, the principal of my school, was honoured by the President of India.

x) **A come is used when some prepositions are used as coordinating conjunctions:**

    A) I cannot attend the meeting, for I am not feeling well.

    B) He was not an accused of murder, but was sentenced to death.

Note: Sometimes misuse of a come may be very fatal:

The District and Session Judge delivered judgement in a murder case.

"To be acquitted not, to be hanged."
But invariably or intentionally typed:
"To be acquitted, not to be hanged."

There is a very interesting story about the misuse of the comma by a typist while typing the judgement delivered by the judge in a murder case.

An old woman's only son was charged with murder and he was to be sentenced to death.

She ran pillar to post to save her son's life at any cost and finding no way out she fell down to the feet of the typist who was living at the next door of her house.

She approached him and requested to save his son's life, she believed only he could do it as he typed the judgement delivered by the judge. She left only after getting firm assurance. The typist was very experienced and intelligent too. Whole night he was restless. He thought and thought and at last he found out a trick to save the life of her only son.

He changed the place of the comma while concluding the judgement in the last paragraph:

In fact, the judgement was as follows: "The accused acquitted not, to be hanged." But he typed - "The accused acquitted, not to be hanged." The defence lawyer argued and her son was acquitted from the charge of murder. Thus a slight change in the place of **a comma saved her son of being hanged.**

3. Sign of Interrogation or Interrogative Sign (?):

It is quite clear that a sign of interrogation is used after every interrogative sentence. First of all the learners ought to be acquainted with the rules of making interrogative sentences, only then they can understand as to how or wherein interrogative signs can be used.

I want to repeat it:

i) **A sentence in which somebody asks or enquires about something from someone is known as Interrogative sentence. For example:**

A) Do you know how to drive a car?

B) Are you going to market?

C) Where are you going now?

D) Have you done your homework?

E) Why have you stolen her pen?

F) Has it been raining outside?

G) Does she sing a song?

H) Did he return your bag?

I) Do you like it?

J) Did they leave for Kolkata?

K) Where did she live these days?

L) Was she teaching her younger brother?

M) Will you buy a book for me?

N) Is he your teacher?

O) Was he a student of our school?

P) Have you a cow in your house?

Q) Has she an umbrella?

R) She is a pretty girl, isn't she?

S) He won the prize? Didn't he?

T) Didn't I warn you? Did I?

U) Didn't she come back? Did she?

V) What is your name?

W) Where do you live at?

X) What is your father?

Y) Who is your father?

Z) Where is your father?

All interrogative sentences begin with auxiliary verbs or interrogative pronouns i.e. where, when, how, who, what, why, whom, which etc.

In all interrogative sentences auxiliary verbs, except in cases of Present Indefinite and Past Indefinite Tenses, precede the subjects or subject alike word/words.

In all assertive sentences of almost all tenses except present indefinite tense and past indefinite tense auxiliary verbs are already there following their subjects.

To convert them into interrogative sentences the places of the auxiliary verbs are to be changed i.e. from the succeeding places to that of preceding places i.e. before the subject or subject alike.

However "Do" or "Does" are used as auxiliary verbs in present indefinite tense and "Did" in the past indefinite tense. "Do" in cases of first person singular and plural number, second person singular and plural number and third person plural number and in case of third person singular number "Does" only is used in order to convert the assertive (Affirmative and Negative Sentences) sentences into interrogative ones. But in the past indefinite tense only "Did" is used in all cases as auxiliary verbs to convert assertive sentences into interrogative ones.

From the examples given above it is clear how to make interrogative sentences in different tenses.

At the end of all such interrogative sentences the signs of interrogation or interrogative signs (?) are used.

I think no more explanation is required to throw light upon interrogative sign.

4. Inverted Commas:

In Direct Speech of narration what is said or quoted by the speaker, when it is exactly indicated or reproduced in his or her language, his or her statement is shown or indicated within inverted commas. For example:

"The earth moves round the Sun." said the teacher.

She said to her mother, "I am going to market now." When a stanza of a poem is quoted or cited for reference, inverted commas are used in the beginning and at the end of it. For instance:

"This be the verse you grave for me,

Here he lies where he longs to be,
Home is the sailor, home from the sea,
And the hunter, home from the hill."
A stanza from the poem – "An Epitaph"
By the poet Robert Louis Stevenson.

Inverted commas are also used to make a word or sentence emphatic in order to draw the attention of the readers:

A) Please grant me casual leave for five days. Here "for" is a preposition.
B) My daughter is not able to attend her class, for she suffers from headache. Here "for" is a conjunction.
C) Our teacher said to us, "The earth moves round the Sun." – Direct Speech.
D) Our teacher told us that the earth goes round the Sun. – Indirect Speech.
   Though the reporting verb "said" is in the past tense, the tense of the reported speech – "The earth moves round the Sun." does not change because the statement made in the reporting speech is a "Universal truth."

The prominent word or sentence is shown within inverted commas in order to draw the attention of the readers.

5 Sign of Exclamation or Interjection: It is used at the end of an exclamatory or interjectional sentences. The exclamatory or interjectional sentence may be a word or a group of words or a sentence with or without complete sense. Since the sense is inherent or hidden or understood even in a single word or a group of words in exclamatory sentence, the necessary factors of a sentence is not required. For example:

A) Amazing!
B) What a win!

C) What a beautiful scene!

D) What a pretty girl she is!

When some of the word/words that comes/come out of the mouth (expressed suddenly in emotion), a sign of exclamation or interjection is used just after it.

These words are used differently in different state of feeing. Each word is specified for a specific nature of emotion or feeling.

    i)   Alas!, oh!, ah! for sorrow or suffering or grief

    ii) Hurrah!- for joy or happiness or pleasure

    iii) Bravo!- for admiration or appreciation

    iv) Ha!, ha!- for amusement

    v) Lo!, hush!- for drawing attention

    vi) What!- for surprise or astonishment

    vii) Fie! Fie! - For contempt or condemn

    viii)Hello! - For greeting or welcoming someone

    ix) Ho! - to call someone to attract his or her attention

Note: a) One important point is worth noting that a sign of exclamation is a must just after the word/words of exclamation and at the same time if it is succeeded by a part of a sentence or by a complete sentence another sign of exclamation is used once again at the end of such a part or a complete sentence.

Note: b) As soon as a sign of exclamation is used just after the word or words of exclamation i.e. Hurrah!, Alas!, Bravo!, Fie! Fie! Etc. and another sentence or a part of a sentence begins with just after, another sign of exclamation is used after the end of such a sentence. Obviously, such a sentence begins with a "capital letter." For example:

A) Bravo! India won the T20 world cup!

B) Alas! We have lost the match!

C) Hello! You are welcome to my new house!

D) What a beautiful scene!

E) Oh! What a fool I am!

6. **Sign of Apostrophe:**

A) It is used to omit a letter or more than a letter with a view to shortening the word/words or form/forms. For example:

- i) Hon'ble from honourable
- ii) Can't for cannot
- iii) Isn't for is not
- iv) Couldn't for could not
- v) Aren't for are not
- vi) I'm for I am
- vii) Won't for will not
- viii) Doesn't for does not
- ix) Don't for do not
  And so on…

Apostrophe is used in Possessive or Genitive case when a noun indicates possession of something. For example:

- i) When it shows possession:
  Mohan's book, Mathew's umbrella, mother's purse etc.
- ii) When a word in singular number ends with s:
  Mathematics' problems, Physics' rule etc.
- iii) When a word in plural number ends with s, only apostrophe is used after these words to show possession:
  Ladies' garments, Ladies' wear, Ladies' beauty parlour, Ladies' seats, Babies' toys, Girls' hostels, Boys' Jims etc.
  But s is used after these words ending with s:
  Venus's glory, James's wits etc.

Caution: No apostrophe is used after these words:
Your's faithfully, - Most of the people use apostrophe after "Your" which is a silly mistake. No apostrophe is used after "Yours." Please make a note of it.
Similarly no apostrophe is used after these words:
Hers, ours, theirs
You can know more about usage of Apostrophe in Possessive or Genitive case in Grammar.

7. **Colon** (:) It is used normally to refer further something more:

   i)   The names of five great leaders are as follows:
        Mahatma Gandhi, Nelson Mandela, Chou En Lie, George Washington
   ii) The following Nobel laureates got the Nobel Prize in literature:
        Rabindranath Tagore, Bertrand Russell, Earnest Hemingway, Pablo
        Neruda

8. **Semicolon**: It shows a little bit less pause than a full stop and a little bit more
pause than a comma. In fact, it is rarely used these days. People use normally
comma instead. Even then it occupies its place in Grammar.

   It is mainly used when one sentence or phrase or group of words of
   similar nature or state follows just after the other. For example:
   I applied for the post; I appeared at the written examination; I faced
   the interview; I was not selected.
   I like rice; I like bread; I like fruits; I can live on anything else.
   I never like smoking; I never like wine; I know these are injurious to
   health.

9. **Dash** (--) **and Hyphen** (-): The dash is used to separate a sentence from one
another or a statement from one another whereas the hyphen is used to separate
one word from other to show a close relation to each other or to one another.

For instance:

   i)   All – the chairman, the principal, the secretary, the parents; students;
        will be present in the annual day function. Here a dash is used.
   ii) A hyphen is used between two numbers while writing them one after
        another from 21 to 99 in words. For instance:
        Fifty-one, Sixty-one, Ninety-nine
        Note: In fact, its use is not in practice. People use to write – Fifty one,
        sixty one, seventy nine. You can check it while people are drawing
        cheques and while writing them in their cheque leaves.
        Truly speaking I am not an exception to these people. I also write
        ignoring the right use of hyphen in such cases.
   iii) A hyphen is used to separate one word from another to show the sense
        or meaning as a whole. For instance:

Father-in-law, mother-in-law, brother-in-law, sister-in-law, Commander-in-chief, Runner-by, Passer-by

In case of compound adjectives a hyphen is used to show the sense together. For instance:

An eleven-storey building, a ready-to-wear garments shop, A ten-days-free-trial- drive

10. **Use of Capital Letters:**

A) The first letter of proper nouns begins with a capital letter.
B) The first word of a sentence begins with a capital letter.
C) Every line of a poem/verse begins with a capital letter.
D) I and O are always written in capital letters irrespective of its place in a sentence.
E) All nouns and the pronouns referring to God but not gods are always written in capital letters.
F) All abbreviations that are used for a larger forms are written in capital letters.
G) All the first letters of the words used as an address in respect or honour of someone are capital letters.
H) The first letter of each word of heading or title of a book or story or institution or organisation or firm or company is capital letter except the prepositions, conjunctions and articles that come in the middle or at the end of such heading or title. For instance:

   i)   The Old Man and the Sea.
   ii)   The Stories from the East and the West
   iii) Indian Institute of Technology
   iv)   Indian Institute of Management
   v)   Lions Clubs International
   vi)   World Health Organisation
   vii) Steel Authority of India

But sometimes each word may begin with a capital letter.

i)   The Old Man And Sea
ii) Indian Institute Of Science

iii) The Good And The Great

    Note: It is argued that the heading or title or name looks better and so it is written in equal order of fashion or design.

11. Bracket:

Bracket is also an important part of Punctuation. Normally it is used in Mathematics. In Algebra (A part of Mathematics) three types of brackets are commonly used. They are as follows:

A) When used as Parentheses: ( )

B) When used as square brackets: [ ]

C) When used as braces: { }

D) When used as an angle brackets: 〈 〉

In Grammar only Parentheses are used in order to emphasise something very important in the middle of a sentence. For example:

A) I (Though not a member of the political party) opposed openly for misuse of public money in advertisement.

    This is the last chapter of E-English Grammar Vol. – I. Very soon you will be able to read the next book – Vol.-II.

    I am sure by this time you have learnt a lot to enrich your knowledge of English language and literature.

*   *   *

About the Author

Name: Durga Prasad

Birth Place: Govindpur, Distt.: Dhanbad (Jharkhand)

Education: B.Com., M.A.- Hindi (Part - I), M.A. (LSW), PGD/M.A. (Human Rights) PGD (Journalism & Mass Communication), Diploma in Business Admn., Bachelor Of Law.

Birth Date: 10th April 1946.

Training: Postal coaching on Story- Writing under the guidance of Dr. Maharaj Krishna Jain, Kahani Lekhan Mahavidyalya, Ambala cant.

Co- Editor of Aasha - Annual Magazine of Lions Club Of Gobindpur.

Worked in different responsible positions and retired as Finance Manager from Central Hospital, B.C.C.L., Dhanbad on 30th. April 2006.

Presently Advocate in Dhanbad Court, Trustee - Lions Club SSMS Eye Hospital, Govindpur, Dhanbad.

Composition: Nearly 50 satire published in the Dainik Jagran, Dhanbad. Many stories published in the local News Paper etc. More than a hundred stories, essays, articles were published in Google Play as E-Blue Books. He has his own website as www.e-bluebooks.com in which almost all his e-blue books are available and can be accessed to on online payment.

Experience of teaching English: The author has got the long teaching experience of teaching English to his wards, students and teachers since 1959 - when he was merely a student of class X of High School, Govindpur, Dhanbad.

He served as Assistant teacher (English) in Govindpur High School from 1964 to 1967. He is still a very good English teacher and spares his valuable time to teach the wards and students of his neighbourhood and nearby places.

*　　*　　*

Printed in the United States
By Bookmasters